GOLD

Eight Stories of the Metal That Redirected Humanity

Nathan Mercer and Peter Hollins

First Edition

Contents

<u>Book One of MATERIALS THAT CHANGED THE WORLD</u>

INTRODUCTION — THE VAULT UNDER LIBERTY STREET

Eighty feet below Liberty Street, a man in steel-toed boots lifts a single gold bar off a pallet, carries it three steps across a locked cage, and sets it down on a pallet that looks exactly the same. He weighs it, notes the number stamped on its side, and moves it from the pile that belongs to one country to the pile that belongs to another. He doesn't know either country. He'll never spend a cent of what he just carried. The bar is worth more than he earns in a year, and the only thing that has changed about it is which cage it sits in.

The man works in the gold vault under the New York Federal Reserve Bank — a basement holding about six thousand tons of the metal, stacked in bars on pallets behind a ninety-ton steel door. By law, almost none of it belongs to the United States. Most of it belongs to the central banks of other countries, and a small share to the International Monetary Fund. None of it has been touched, beyond that kind of careful shuffling, in decades. It earns no interest and no return. Its worth, at the prices of late 2025, is more than half a trillion dollars.

Climb to the upper floors of the same building, and you will find the people who run the world's money. They haven't used gold to back a currency since 1971. They don't need to. They have computers, treaties, satellite links, and a web of trust between governments that didn't exist in any earlier century of human history.

And yet the gold is still in the basement. Every country that put it there has had many chances, over the last half-century, to take it home or to sell it. None of them have done so. The metal simply sits where it sits.

This book is about that metal.

Gold has done one thing again and again for human beings, in every culture and every century where it has been used: it turns them. Emperors, friars, conquistadors, doges, prospectors, and queens have all been turned by it. Gold has caused choices that the people making them wouldn't have made for any other reason. It has bent the path of the empires that made them — sometimes toward ruin, sometimes toward what those people thought of as the better. And the cost was always paid by someone other than the one reaching for it.

The metal itself is good for almost nothing. You can't eat it, and it builds nothing that other stuff couldn't build for less. It's too soft for tools, too heavy for armor, too rare to be money on a large scale, too dead for chemistry. Nearly all we have done with gold has been for show, for worship, for money, or for meaning — a worth we made up, not one we dug out.

And yet we have made it up so steadily, across so many centuries and so many cultures, that gold is one of the very few things every people seems to crave. The Egyptians worked it and the Chinese taxed in it. The Inca poured it into temple walls, and the Vikings stole it from monasteries. In Rome the Catholic Church took it for indulgences, and the Bank of England held it against the pound. The Russian central bank stored it up against the day of sanctions. Even Bitcoin, built in 2008 as a way around state money, gets called digital gold by the people who hold it.

What follows is a book of eight stories. There is no narrative running from one to the next, and they build toward no sweeping verdict on how gold made or unmade the great powers. Every one is its own complete drama — a king, a queen, a city, a friar, a conquistador, a mountain, a carpenter. And each one shows the reader a single example of what gold can do when human beings get close to it.

The eight stories span twenty-four hundred years, from the kingdom of Lydia in the sixth century BC to the foothills of the Sierra Nevada in the nineteenth century AD. They take place in eight different cities on four continents. The people in them speak Lydian, Greek, Latin, Quechua, Persian, Arabic, German, Spanish, and the tongues of half a dozen empires that are gone. They die in palaces, on funeral pyres, in tombs, in market squares, in mineshafts, in hotel rooms, and in cabins on the side of stripped-out hills. They're joined by nothing except the metal that drew them in.

All of it comes back to gold. Not because the metal is interesting on its own — it isn't — but because of what it has done, over and over, to the people who end up in the same room with it.

What you're holding is a string of episodes. Each one is true. They were set down by chroniclers who were there, or who spoke to people who were. Any of them is short enough to read in an afternoon by someone who has never given the subject a thought. That gold sits at the center of them all is the only reason for putting them in the same book.

The metal is still in the basement under Liberty Street. The Federal Reserve doesn't show it off, and there are no tours. The vault was last sorted in 1989. Most of it's the same gold that was placed there in the 1930s and 1940s. Europe and Asia were on fire then, and central banks moved their reserves to a country they thought would still be standing when the smoke cleared.

It's still there because everyone with a claim on it would rather it stay in a vault on Liberty Street than go anywhere else. That shared choice is an unspoken pact: the gold will stay put, won't be sold, won't be used, but will simply go on sitting. And it's the same deal, in a slightly more sophisticated form, that Croesus first asked the citizens of Sardis to enter into in 547 BCE.

The deal has held, with some interruptions, for twenty-four hundred years.

The eight chapters that follow are about the interruptions.

CHAPTER ONE — THE KING WHO INVENTED MONEY

Money is an agreement. The man who first asked others to enter it was one of its earliest victims.

Sardis, Lydia, c. 560–547 BCE

The mint at Sardis was hot. In the corner a clay furnace glowed orange, fed by a boy with a leather bellows. At the anvil the smith drew a small disc of metal from the coals with iron tongs, dropped it into place, and brought down a heavy stamp — two strikes, one for each side. When he lifted the stamp away, the disc bore a snarling lion's head on the front and a charging bull on the back. The king who stood watching beside him was, at that moment, the richest man in the world.

His name was Croesus, and he was about to become richer still.

The coin on the anvil was the first of its kind. It was made of pure gold — not electrum, the muddy yellow mix of gold and silver that his father's mint had struck for two lifetimes, but real, clean gold. The Lydians had only lately learned to win it from the silver, and now it carried his royal mark. That mark was the whole point. A trader in the market no longer had to weigh the coin or bite it, no longer had to argue with the seller about whether the metal was pure. The lion and the bull said everything: this disc has the king's word on it, and the king says it's worth what it says it's worth. It was a small thing, a piece of metal the size of a thumbnail. But in its quiet way, it was the beginning of the modern world.

Lydia sat where it had always sat — a wedge of land in what's today western Turkey, between the Greek cities on the coast and the great empires of the east. Through it ran a small river called the Pactolus, which carried gold dust down from the mountains. The Greeks had a story about that river. Long ago, they said, a king named Midas had washed himself in the Pactolus to wash off his own curse, the curse of turning everything he touched to gold. The gold he washed away had stayed in the river ever since. The myth was a story; the gold was real.

For hundreds of years the Lydians had panned the Pactolus, much as later prospectors would pan the rivers of California — squatting in the shallows, swirling sand in flat wooden trays, watching the heavy yellow flakes settle to the bottom. That alone had made the Lydian kings rich.

But the real breakthrough came in the years before Croesus took the throne. Lydian metalworkers learned how to separate gold from silver. Nature gave them electrum in mixed lumps, and they found a way to split it cleanly into its two metals. The method was called cementation. They heated the electrum with salt in a clay pot, slowly, for many hours. The salt drew the silver out of the metal and held onto it. What was left behind was gold of a purity no one had ever held in his hand. For the next fifteen hundred years, alchemists would chase a grander prize — turning cheap base metal like lead into gold — and they would always fail, because it can't be done by fire and salt. The Lydians' trick was the closest anyone ever got: not magic, but the real chemistry of pulling one metal cleanly out of another. This was the skill that made Croesus possible. Once you could separate gold from silver, you could mint coins of known worth. Once you could mint coins of known worth, the king could put his name on them. And once the king could put his name on them, money — real money, in the modern sense — existed.

Croesus took the throne around 560 BCE, at roughly thirty-five years old. With it came the gold of the Pactolus, the trade routes to the Greek coast, and the new coinage his father had begun. Within a few years he had grown all of it. He conquered the Greek cities of the Ionian coast and swept their wealth into his treasury. He paid to rebuild the great temple of Artemis at Ephesus, which would later be counted among the seven wonders of the ancient world. And he won over the great kings of his time — the pharaohs of Egypt, the rulers of Babylon — by sending them gifts of gold so huge that no one could politely refuse.

He filled his palace with gold thrones, gold drinking cups, and gold bars stacked like firewood in the treasure vaults. His wealth became a legend while he was still living. The phrase "rich as Croesus" outlived every empire of his age. People still use it today, twenty-five hundred years later, people who have never heard of him.

One of his visitors during these good years was a man from Athens named Solon, already old, one of the great lawmakers of the Greek world. He had given the Athenians the basic shape of their laws, and he was traveling now because he had asked his own people to leave those laws untouched for ten years, and they had agreed. Croesus collected famous men the way he collected gold. He brought Solon to the palace and led him through the vaults, past the chests of coin and the bars stacked floor to ceiling, past every treasure the eastern world had to offer. At the end of it he couldn't help himself. He turned to Solon and asked the question he had been waiting to ask. Tell me, he said. In all your travels, who's the happiest man you have ever met?

He was expecting one answer. He was expecting Solon to say: You, Croesus. You're the happiest man I have ever met.

Solon didn't say that.

Instead he named an ordinary citizen of Athens, a man who had lived an honest life, had seen his sons grow up well, and had died in battle for his city. The happiest man, Solon said, is the man who's already dead and beyond the reach of fortune, for no man can be called happy until his life is over and the story is whole. Until then, anything can still go wrong. Croesus sent him away, out of Sardis, and went on being the richest man in the world.

He forgot.

Some years later he began to think about Persia. To his east a new power was rising. A man named Cyrus had taken the throne of the Medes, then conquered them. Now he was welding together a Persian empire that already stretched from the Caspian Sea to the borders of India. Croesus could feel that growth the way a small kingdom always feels a large one swelling on its border. He decided to strike first, before Cyrus came to him. But he was a careful man, and he wanted to be sure he would win. So he tested the gods.

He sent messengers to every great oracle in the Greek world. Each carried sealed orders to ask the same thing on the same day — the hundredth day after leaving Sardis. The question was simple: what's the king of Lydia doing right now? It was a trap. On that day, alone in his palace kitchens, Croesus chopped up a tortoise and a lamb and boiled them together in a bronze pot with a bronze lid. No god or man could have known that. The reports came back one by one, and every oracle but one guessed wrong. Only Delphi, the oracle of Apollo, answered right, in verse:

> I count the sands and measure the sea,
> I hear the silent and know the dumb.
> I scent the smell of the hard-shelled tortoise,
> Boiled in bronze with the flesh of the lamb.

Croesus was pleased. Delphi knew everything. He sent the oracle a thank-you gift worthy of him: 117 bars of solid gold, each one heavy enough to need two men to lift it. There was a solid gold lion the size of a small child. There was a statue of a baker-woman cast in pure gold, four and a half feet tall. There were bowls of silver and bowls of gold by the dozen — so much that the treasury at Delphi groaned under the weight of it. Only then did he send his real question. Should he attack the Persians? The answer came back in a single line: if Croesus crosses the river Halys, he will destroy a great empire. He read it twice. A great empire would be destroyed. That was all he needed to know.

In the spring of 547 BCE Croesus crossed the Halys at the head of his army and marched east into Cappadocia. He met Cyrus on a plain near a place called Pteria. The two armies bled through a full day of fighting, and at dusk both fell back to their camps with no winner. Croesus had expected an easy victory and hadn't gotten one, and worse, his army was smaller than he had imagined. He had counted on Egyptian and Babylonian allies who hadn't yet come. So he decided to fall back to Sardis for the winter, gather his strength, and try again in the spring with his whole alliance behind him.

It was a reasonable decision. It was the wrong one.

Cyrus didn't wait for the spring. He marched his army across the high Anatolian plateau in winter, through cold and snow and country no army was supposed to cross in that season. He reached the gates of Sardis before Croesus had finished sending his hired soldiers home. That left Croesus with only his core force. The heart of that force was its cavalry, and the Lydian cavalry was the finest in the eastern world: armored riders on huge horses, trained from boyhood for the lance and the charge. Cyrus had ridden against them once already and knew he had no answer for them. So he made one.

He had learned something in his years on the steppes. Horses will put up with almost any other animal, but they lose their nerve at the smell of a camel. Cyrus had camels in his baggage train carrying supplies. He ordered them stripped of their packs, mounted with his lightest soldiers, and lined up at the front of his battle line. When the Lydian cavalry charged, the horses smelled the camels and reared, throwing their riders and bolting back the way they had come, trampling the Lydian foot soldiers behind them. By the time the Lydians had formed up again on foot, they were already beaten.

Croesus pulled back inside the walls of Sardis. The walls were huge, built into the side of a mountain so steep that one face of the city was thought to be unclimbable. He had food and supplies for years. He sent runners to Egypt, to Sparta, to Babylon, asking for help.

The siege lasted fourteen days.

On the fourteenth day, a Lydian soldier on the unclimbable face of the wall dropped his helmet. It rolled and bounced down the slope, and the soldier, against orders, climbed down after it. A Persian watching from below saw the route he took. That night Persian raiders followed the same route up the slope, hand over hand in the dark, finding the cracks and ledges the Lydian had shown them. By dawn they were inside the city.

Croesus was taken alive.

What happened next is the part of the story the Greeks couldn't stop telling. Cyrus had decided to burn the captured king. Some sources say it was an offering to his gods. Others say it was a test, to see whether the gods would step in for the most famous man on earth. His soldiers built a great pyre in the square at Sardis, tied Croesus to a post on top of it, and lit the wood at the corners. Croesus, standing in the rising smoke, called out three times: Solon. Solon. Solon.

Cyrus, watching from below, asked his interpreter what the word meant. The interpreter asked the king on the pyre. With the fire climbing toward him, Croesus told the story of the Athenian who had once warned him that no man could be called happy until he was dead. He had laughed at the warning, and forgotten it, and was remembering it now. Cyrus was a thoughtful man as well as a great conqueror. He looked at the burning pyre and at the king on top of it, and he saw himself — a man too, whose own luck could turn. He ordered the fire put out.

But the fire had taken hold and wouldn't die. According to Herodotus, Croesus then prayed to Apollo. The god, pleased with all the gold he had once been given at Delphi, sent a sudden rainstorm that drowned the flames. Croesus was untied and brought down. He spent the rest of his life as an advisor at the court of Cyrus.

In his quieter years he's said to have sent priests back to Delphi to demand an answer. The oracle replied, calmly, that it had been right. He had crossed the river, and a great empire had indeed been destroyed. The oracle had simply not said whose. That's the story the Greeks told, and it became a kind of lesson. In the writing of the centuries that followed, Croesus became every man who reached for too much because he had heard what he wanted to hear.

But the parable isn't the only thing he left behind.

When Cyrus took Sardis, he kept the mint. He kept the cementation furnaces, the smiths, and the dies that stamped the lion and the bull. He kept the whole system of putting a king's mark on a clean disc of metal and sending it out into the world. The Persian Empire was now growing in every direction, and it took the Lydian coinage as its own. The Persian gold daric and silver siglos paid the Persian army and tax officials for the next two hundred years. They came straight from the coin Croesus had watched come off the anvil at Sardis.

From Persia the system spread west. The Greek cities began striking their own coins on the Lydian model — the silver owl of Athens chief among them. When Alexander the Great set out to conquer the known world, he paid his armies in coined silver. The Romans took over his eastern empire, and they kept the system too; the denarius of imperial Rome was a Lydian coin in everything but name. Every great civilization that came after has used coined money, stamped by some ruling power. The medieval Christian and Islamic worlds used it, and so did the kingdoms of India and China that traded with them, the European empires of the modern age, and every nation on earth today. All of it comes straight from the lion-and-bull stater struck in the mint at Sardis.

Without that coin, the empires that came after couldn't have existed. You can't pay a standing army in lumps of metal that must be weighed and tested at every deal. You can't collect taxes from a province a thousand miles away in cattle or grain. And you can't run a city full of strangers without some thing that everyone, everywhere, agrees is worth what it says it's worth. That thing didn't exist before Croesus. It has existed ever since.

The empire he destroyed by crossing the river was his own. The empire he founded by stamping a coin hasn't ended. It's on every screen you check, every card you swipe, every bill in every wallet and every number in every account. And it began, more or less, with a lion and a bull, struck on a small hot disc, by a man who would soon ride out of Sardis and lose everything that mattered to him.

Alexandria, August 30 BCE.

Five centuries after the lion and the bull, the largest treasury the Mediterranean had ever held stood unguarded behind an open door.

CHAPTER TWO — THE TREASURY THAT BUILT ROME

An empire is paid for. The treasury that funds it has, almost always, belonged to someone else.

Alexandria and Rome, 30–27 BCE

The doors of the palace at Alexandria stood open, and there was no one left to close them. The young man who walked through them on a hot August morning in 30 BCE was thirty-three years old, slight, blond, often sickly, and almost entirely without armor. There was no one left in the city who would have raised a hand against him. Octavian was the great-nephew and adopted heir of the murdered Julius Caesar, and for fourteen years he had been fighting a civil war for the Roman world. Now the war was over, and the last of his rivals lay dead in the rooms beyond the courtyard.

The treasury of the Ptolemies was unlocked, unguarded, and waiting for him. It held three hundred years of gold gathered by the Greek family that had ruled Egypt since Alexander the Great. Beneath that lay the older wealth of the pharaohs, going back two thousand years before that.

He walked through the rooms in silence. He looked at it.

The vaults were colder than the air outside. The gold was stacked on shelves and in chests and in heaps on the floors — coined gold, hammered gold, gold in plate and bar and ornament. It was the gifts of pharaohs and the savings of a Greek family that had taxed the Nile for ten generations.

What he saw in those rooms would, within ten years, fund the deepest reshaping of any city in the old world. It would lower the interest rate in Rome from twelve percent to four percent almost overnight, and it would pay and calm a standing army of three hundred thousand men who had been close to mutiny over unpaid wages. It would rebuild the streets, temples, and forums of the city he was about to rename for himself. And against everyone's hopes and fears, it would establish two hundred years of unbroken peace from the British Isles to Mesopotamia. The Pax Romana — the longest stretch of calm in the West's history — began, in a real sense, in the rooms Octavian walked through that morning.

It began with a woman who had killed herself rather than walk behind his triumph.

Octavian's war was old news. By the summer of 30 BCE, it had been grinding on for fourteen years. It had begun with the murder of Julius Caesar on the floor of the Senate in 44 BCE. It had pulled in every ambitious man in the Roman world: Marc Antony, who had been Caesar's right hand and friend, and Octavian himself, the unknown boy Caesar had named in his will. The old Republican holdouts went down in battle in 42 BCE. After that the war narrowed to a duel between the two men left standing — Antony in the east, Octavian in the west, the Roman general and the Roman heir.

By the late 30s BC, the western half of the Roman world belonged to Octavian, and the eastern half belonged to Antony. Antony had made his home in Alexandria, in the court of Cleopatra, the last Ptolemaic queen of Egypt. By birth she was a Greek, by title a pharaoh. And by all accounts she was the one person in the eastern Mediterranean both rich enough and clever enough to fund Antony's claim to Rome. She had borne him three children and backed him in gold and grain, letting him use her treasury as if it were his own.

That was the problem. The treasury wasn't his own. It was hers.

Octavian, in Rome, didn't need to spell out the danger. Everyone could see what it would mean for the

Republic if Antony came back to claim the city with an Egyptian fortune behind him. So Octavian simply made sure that Romans saw it. He seized Antony's will from the Vestal Virgins, the Roman priestesses who guarded important documents, where Antony had left it for safekeeping, and read it aloud in the Senate. The will said that Antony wished to be buried in Alexandria, beside Cleopatra. To a Roman crowd that was the same as saying Antony had stopped being Roman. He had gone eastern, soft, slavish — a man who had given himself to a foreign queen. The Senate declared war not on Antony, but on Cleopatra.

The two fleets met on the second of September, 31 BCE, off the coast of western Greece, at a low rocky point called Actium. It was a strange, half-hearted battle, in which Antony's larger ships were outsailed by Octavian's smaller, faster ones. In the middle of the afternoon, before the outcome was clear, the Egyptian ships under Cleopatra's own command turned south. They set their sails and ran for it, breaking through the line of battle and out into open water. Antony, seeing his queen leave, gave up his own flagship and followed her in a small fast galley. Whatever they were running toward, it wasn't victory.

By nightfall the rest of the Roman ships on Antony's side had given up. The eastern half of the Roman world fell to Octavian without a second battle.

The treasury he had been fighting for was now a few weeks' sail away, in a city he had never seen.

Antony and Cleopatra had ten months left.

They fell back to Alexandria and tried to make a deal. Cleopatra sent envoys to Octavian, offering to give up the throne for her children if some part of the Ptolemaic line could be left on the throne. Octavian sent polite replies that promised nothing. He was in no hurry. He could let the queen sit in her palace with her vaults untouched for one more year, as long as the vaults didn't move. He spent the winter in Asia Minor, gathered fresh troops in the spring, and began his march on Egypt in the summer of 30 BCE. By the end of July his legions were at the gates of Alexandria.

Antony's last troops went over to Octavian without a fight. Antony was told that Cleopatra had killed herself. The report was false; she had locked herself in her own tomb and sent word out to confuse him. He fell on his sword. He didn't die at once. His servants found him bleeding on the floor. When they learned that the queen was still alive after all, they carried him to her tomb. She wouldn't unbolt the door, so they lifted him in through an upper window on ropes. He died in her arms a few hours later.

Cleopatra was thirty-nine years old. She had ruled Egypt for twenty-one years. She had borne four children, three of them to Antony, one — the oldest — to Julius Caesar. She had been the consort of two of the most powerful men in the Roman world. When Octavian's soldiers broke open her tomb, they took her alive and kept her in the palace under guard.

Octavian visited her once and was, his biographers report, cold. He meant to take her to Rome in chains and march her behind his triumph, in the usual Roman way, as a live trophy of his win. She understood this well. On the tenth of August, 30 BCE, she dressed in her full royal robes and had her two servants do the same. Then she ate from a basket of figs that had been brought to the palace that morning. Inside the basket, by the best-known version of the story, was a small Egyptian cobra. She let it bite her on the arm. By the time Octavian's guards broke down the door, she was dead in her chair, on her throne, in the clothes of a queen.

She had cheated him of his triumph.

The next thing Octavian did was kill Caesarion.

Caesarion was seventeen years old. He was Cleopatra's eldest son, and he was, by every report, the only blood son Julius Caesar had ever had. Cleopatra had sent him south, toward India, with a keeper and a small store of gold, hoping to get him out of the country before Octavian arrived. Octavian's agents found him on the road, lured him back with false promises of safe travel, and put him to death. To one of his men, Octavian is said to have put it in a Greek phrase that means, roughly: too many Caesars is no good thing.

It was a careful murder, and it mattered. Octavian's whole legal claim on the Roman world rested on being Caesar's adopted heir. A living blood son of Caesar was a threat to a throne Octavian hadn't yet formally taken. It didn't matter that the boy was an Egyptian who had never set foot in Italy. With Caesarion dead, no rival claim to Caesar's name was left in any corner of the Roman world.

There was now only the gold.

The treasury of the Ptolemies was the largest store of refined gold and silver in the ancient world.

It had been built up over three hundred years by the Greek family that ruled Egypt. They had taken power when one of Alexander the Great's generals seized the country in 323 BCE. From that day they held the farm wealth of the Nile valley — the richest grain land in the Mediterranean. They taxed it hard, saved the takings, and pulled in more gold from the mines of Nubia and the trade routes of the Red Sea. They stacked it in vaults beneath their palaces and spent it sparingly. Now and then they showed it off in festivals so grand that the Greek world remembered them for hundreds of years.

On top of that Ptolemaic wealth lay the older treasure of Egypt itself. This was gold gathered by the pharaohs across two thousand years. It was mined from Nubia and the eastern desert. It was taken from the grave goods of robbed tombs and taxed from a people who knew no other way to live. To picture it, think of the gold burial mask of the boy-king Tutankhamun, found untouched in 1922 — twenty-two pounds of solid gold over one dead face. The treasure Octavian walked through was that kind of gold, gathered across two thousand years and a hundred such tombs. Some of it sat in the temple vaults, the gifts of many generations of worshippers. Some of it was the jewelry of dead queens. Some of it had been buried, dug up, melted down, and buried again so many times that no one could now name where it came from. All of it was now Octavian's.

He took it carefully and in order. The Ptolemaic vaults he seized whole. The temples he stripped of their gold gifts. From the noble houses of Alexandria he took what could be taken, by polite request where he could and by force where he couldn't. Then he had the gold loaded onto ships — Roman warships and seized Egyptian trading boats. He sent it west across the Mediterranean to the port of Ostia, at the mouth of the Tiber. What arrived there in the late summer and autumn of 30 BCE was the single greatest move of wealth in the history of the ancient world.

In Rome the effect was immediate and visible.

A Roman biographer, writing a century later from records still open to him, set down the numbers. Interest rates in Rome fell from twelve percent to four percent within months of the gold's arrival. That rate was the price Roman lenders charged Roman borrowers to lend them money. Say a merchant had signed a loan in the spring at the old rate. The price of money had crashed. For its remaining years, that loan was now three times richer for the lender than it had any right to be.

Roman land prices shot up. Romans who held cash now had three times as much buying power per coin, and they bid against each other for the same fields and houses. A small landowner outside the city might wake up to a strange new sum. On paper his little farm was now worth what a senator's estate had been worth a year before. A merchant who had been struggling with the cost of credit suddenly found bankers chasing him to lend.

This is the way a great flood of gold works. The metal itself does nothing. But the moment there's more of it about, every contract and every price recalibrates around its new abundance. The people who were owed gold grew quietly richer. The people who were owed goods or labor grew quietly poorer. The slaves, the city poor, the small farmers of Italy — no one asked them.

For Octavian, none of this was a side effect. It was the design.

The gold did three things at once. First, it paid his legions. They were owed back wages from ten years of war and had been on the edge of mutiny. Now each soldier was paid, and paid well, in fresh coin, and his loyalty was now Octavian's.

Second, it funded a huge new building plan in Rome itself. A new forum. A temple promised in advance to avenge the murder of Julius Caesar. The repair of eighty-two damaged or shabby temples. Paved roads, new aqueducts, public baths, and marble laid over each great building that had once been plain brick. Octavian would say of this work, late in his life — by then under the name Augustus — that he had found Rome a city of brick and left it a city of marble. The marble had come, in the end, from Cleopatra. Third, the gold gave him a steady yearly income, because Octavian ruled that Egypt would no longer be an ordinary part of the Roman Republic. Egypt would belong to the emperor alone.

No Roman senator could enter Egypt without Octavian's express leave. The governor of Egypt wasn't a senator at all but a knight. He was named by the emperor himself, and he answered only to the emperor. The yearly grain harvest of the Nile delta, which fed perhaps one-third of the city of Rome, flowed not into the public treasury but into the emperor's. The taxes of Egyptian farmers didn't pay for Roman roads or Roman wars in the usual Roman way. They paid for the emperor.

This setup began as a short-term way to handle an odd conquest. Then it stayed for good. For the next three hundred years, each emperor of Rome owned Egypt the way a man might own a farm. The grain ships from Alexandria fed the city crowds and kept them from riots. The gold of the Nile valley paid for the royal court and the royal wars. When emperors ran short of money they leaned on Egypt. When they needed troops they paid for them with Egyptian gold.

When they raised monuments they used Egyptian wealth to do it. It's one of the quieter secrets of how Rome really worked, hidden behind the speeches and the wars and the family murders. And it began in the rooms Octavian walked through that summer in Alexandria.

Three years later, in January of 27 BCE, the Roman Senate gave him a new name.

He had already been named imperator, the top army commander. He had already been granted tribunicia potestas, the powers of a tribune of the people. He had already taken hold of the army, the treasury, the grain supply, and the provinces. The Senate had no real choice in the matter. But it was eager to dress the new order in fine clothes, and so it voted to give him a holy title: Augustus. It meant something like the revered one — the sacred, the blessed. It was a name with no real power in it at all, and that was the point. It said simply that he was no longer one Roman among others.

The name was his for the next forty-one years. With great public ceremony he handed the formal powers of the Republic back to the Senate, and quietly kept the real ones. He didn't call himself king. He didn't need to. The treasury was full, the legions were paid, and the Senate could be talked round.

What he built with that gold and that quiet power got a name from the writers who lived inside it. They called it the Pax Romana — the Roman Peace. From the year of his renaming until the death of the emperor Marcus Aurelius in 180 CE, the Roman world was free of major civil war. For two hundred years, a person could travel from Hadrian's Wall in northern Britain to the Euphrates river in modern Iraq. The whole way, there was one law, one coinage, one tax system, and one army to keep the peace. There has never been one more such stretch in Western history. The thousand years after Augustus — Byzantine, medieval, Renaissance, modern — have all looked back to him as the model of what a steady empire could be.

In later ages, historians and Christians argued over why Rome had lasted as long as it did. They tended to credit Roman order, Roman law, Roman building, and Roman religion. They almost never named where the actual money came from. The Augustan Peace, the marble forums, the soldiers' pay, the grain that kept the poor of Rome quiet for two hundred years — all of it had one source. It was paid for, in the end, by what had been taken out of the Ptolemaic treasury in the summer of 30 BCE.

The woman whose death paid for the empire that defined Europe was reduced, in Western memory, to a play. Shakespeare wrote her, and Hollywood costumed her. Schoolchildren today learn her name as a love story, not as an accountant's footnote on the founding of the Roman world.

The empire was the inheritance. She was the price.

The walls of Constantinople, April 1204.

The empire Augustus had built had been moved east twelve centuries earlier; its walls were about to fail for the first time.

CHAPTER THREE — THE CITY THE CHRISTIANS SACKED

Debts are heavier than vows. A journey ends where the men with the ships decide it ends.

Constantinople, April 1204

April thirteenth, 1204. A Venetian galley nosed up to the foot of Constantinople's seawall, its ropes tangling with the wrecks of older defenses. At its prow stood the blind Doge of Venice, Enrico Dandolo, an old man in armor — white-bearded, in red robes over his mail. The eye-slits of his helmet were closed, because the eyes inside no longer worked. He was somewhere past ninety years old, and he was leading the second attack on the largest Christian city in the world.

By the next day the walls would be broken. By the day after that, the city behind them would be in the hands of Western Christians. It held eight centuries of churches and palaces and libraries and treasure — the seat of Orthodox Christendom, the richest concentration of gold and gemwork in the Mediterranean world.

They had set out, six years earlier, to retake Jerusalem from the Muslims. They never reached it. A debt turned them aside.

In August of 1198, Pope Innocent III called for a new Crusade. He was newly chosen, thirty-seven years old, the most driven pope of the Middle Ages. The three earlier Crusades had failed to hold Jerusalem. Innocent wanted a Fourth, and he wanted it done right. He aimed it not at the Holy Land itself but at Egypt, the Muslim state that ruled both Cairo and Jerusalem. Take Cairo, the thinking went, and Jerusalem would follow.

The Crusade needed two things: Christian knights, and ships to carry them.

The knights came in. Across France and the German lands, in 1199 and 1200, nobles took the cross. Their leader, after some bargaining, was an Italian-French count with good connections across Europe. By the spring of 1201 an army of French, Italian, and German Crusaders was gathering. The ships, however, had to be bought.

Only one place in the medieval Christian world could deliver the kind of fleet a Crusade needed, and that place was Venice. The Venetian Republic was a sea city, half-built on water. Its shipyards could lay down hulls faster than any rival in Europe, and its merchant ships already controlled most trade in the Mediterranean. Best of all, its government — the Doge and his council — could be dealt with as a state.

In April 1201, six Crusader envoys arrived at the Venetian Doge's palace. One of them would later write the chronicle that tells us most of what happened. They were brought before the Doge: a man named Enrico Dandolo, then in his nineties. He had been blind for at least twenty years, from a head injury he had taken on a mission to Constantinople long before. The blindness, by every report, hadn't touched his mind or his nerve.

The Crusaders made their request. They needed passage for 33,500 men, 4,500 horses, and a year's supplies, from Venice to Egypt. Dandolo listened and talked it over with his council. He agreed to provide a fleet large enough for that force, plus 50 Venetian warships to guard them — a gift from Venice itself. The price was 85,000 silver marks, to be paid in parts over the next year. It was, by any measure of the medieval world, a vast sum. It came to roughly half the whole yearly income of the kingdom of England. The envoys signed. They had no way of paying it.

They had assumed the Crusader army would be larger than it turned out to be, and that nobles across Europe would answer the call more eagerly than they did. They had assumed, too, that the men who came would bring their own money. By the summer of 1202, the army gathered at Venice and camped on a sandy island at the mouth of the lagoon. By then it was clear that no more than a third of the expected force had come. The money collected from them came to barely two-thirds of what was owed.

Venice had already done the work. The ships were built and waiting. The supplies were piled in the docks. The whole city had been on a war footing for over a year. Dandolo had spent his life weighing risk and reward. He wasn't going to let the Crusaders walk away from the deal. He made them an offer.

The city of Zara sat on the Dalmatian coast, in what's now Croatia. It had belonged to Venice until a decade earlier, when it broke away and put itself under the king of Hungary. The Venetians wanted it back. But the king of Hungary was a Catholic Christian, and Zara was a Catholic Christian city. Attacking it would mean Western Christians sacking Western Christians under the banner of a Crusade. Still, the gold problem was the gold problem. Dandolo proposed that the Crusader army, on its way to Egypt, turn aside to Zara and take it for Venice. The debt would wait until the

Crusade was done. The Crusader leaders saw no other choice, and they agreed.

In November of 1202, the army the Pope had sent to win back Jerusalem sacked the Christian city of Zara. The first siege of the Fourth Crusade was Christian against Christian. When word reached Pope Innocent in Rome, he threw the whole expedition out of the Church. The Crusaders begged forgiveness, and he later took most of them back. But not the Venetians, who weren't sorry. The Crusade wintered in the ruins of Zara, in disgrace. It couldn't go forward, and it couldn't go home.

It was during that winter at Zara that the next offer arrived.

A young man named Alexios Angelos appeared in the Crusader camp. He was the son of Isaac II, the former Byzantine emperor of Constantinople. Seven years before, Isaac's own brother had thrown him off the throne and blinded him. That uncle now sat on the Byzantine throne. Young Alexios had escaped to the West and had been moving from court to court, begging for help to put his father back.

What he offered the Crusaders was the answer to all of their problems at once. Let them turn from Egypt and sail to Constantinople. There they would put his father back on the throne and set him beside his father as co-emperor. In return he would pay them 200,000 silver marks — more than twice the first Venetian debt. He would give the Crusade 10,000 Byzantine troops to join the march on Egypt, and feed and supply the army for a year. And he would do something the popes had wanted for a hundred and fifty years. He would place the Orthodox Church of the East under the Roman pope. That would end the split that had divided Christianity since 1054.

It was a dream. He had no money to back any of these promises, no army to call on, and no power over the Orthodox Church. But the Crusaders didn't know that. The leaders met. Dandolo was the only one among them who had been to Constantinople and knew the city, and he told them to take the deal. Many of the common soldiers said no. They had taken the cross for Jerusalem, not for a fight over the Byzantine throne. Part of the army peeled off and went home. The rest sailed for Constantinople in the spring of 1203.

They arrived off the city in late June.

Nothing any man in the Crusader fleet had ever seen had prepared him for Constantinople. It was the largest city in the Christian world by three times over. Its people numbered somewhere between four and five hundred thousand. Paris, at the time, had perhaps fifty thousand. Its outer walls — the Theodosian walls, built eight centuries earlier — were the strongest in Europe. They had never been broken in their long history. Its churches were roofed in lead and topped in gold. Above the skyline rose the dome of the Hagia Sophia, twice the height of any cathedral the Crusaders had ever seen. A great iron chain, stretched between two towers, closed off the mouth of the harbor.

The Byzantines didn't know what to make of the Crusaders. The would-be emperor Alexios IV was paraded along the seawall on a galley flying his colors. The hope was that the people of Constantinople would know their lost prince and rise up to welcome him. They didn't. The city had mostly forgotten him. The Byzantines weren't in the habit of changing sides to suit Latin invaders.

The Crusaders attacked in July. They broke the harbor chain, landed troops, and set fire to part of the city, and the reigning uncle fled in the night with what gold he could carry. The old, blind Isaac II was now back on the throne. He sent word to the Crusaders that his son could indeed be crowned as co-emperor, and Alexios IV was crowned in August 1203.

He couldn't pay.

His uncle had emptied the treasury. The Orthodox Church refused, of course, to bow to Rome. The 10,000 Byzantine soldiers couldn't be raised. To find the silver he had promised, Alexios IV taxed the city harder than it had been taxed in living memory. He stripped the lead from church roofs. He melted down silver and gold icons and pried gemstones from holy vessels — the most shameful thing a Byzantine emperor could do. He shipped the goods to the Crusaders in their camp across the Golden Horn.

It wasn't enough. By January of 1204, Constantinople was in revolt. A noble nicknamed Murtzuphlos — bushy-eyebrows — led the uprising. Alexios IV was seized, dragged from the palace, and strangled in a dungeon. Isaac II died soon after (some sources say of grief, some say killed). Murtzuphlos was crowned emperor in his place and ordered the Crusaders to leave.

The Crusaders hadn't been paid, and without payment they had no way home. So, in their camp outside the walls of Constantinople, they met in council and decided to take the city.

The first assault, on April 9, 1204, failed against the seawall. The second, on April 12, didn't. High winds, Venetian engineering, and two ships that managed to lash themselves together carried a small band of Crusaders over a tower. Once they were inside, they opened a gate, and the rest of the army poured in.

Constantinople had stood against attackers for eight hundred and seventy-four years. It had held off Arab and Persian armies and a dozen others. It fell, in the end, to fellow Christians with siege ladders and ship-mounted bridges, led by a blind Venetian who had given his last years to the bargain that brought them there.

For three days, the Crusaders sacked the city.

Before the fleet sailed, Pope Innocent III had given strict orders. Christian holy places weren't to be robbed. The Crusader leaders had agreed to the order. The Crusaders themselves, once inside the walls, ignored it completely.

A Byzantine historian, Nicetas Choniates, was in the city through all of it. He lost his own house, and he wrote down what he saw. Crusaders broke into churches and stripped the gold from the altars. They pried open the imperial tombs, including the tomb of Justinian, and from bodies that had lain undisturbed for six hundred years they stole the burial robes and jewels. Holy icons smashed. Neighborhoods that the old empresses had chosen for their summer palaces set on fire. Women dragged out of the churches where they had taken shelter, boys sold into the slave markets that ran in the Crusader camp.

Then there was the Hagia Sophia, the great church of Orthodox Christianity, larger than any building in Western Europe. Its dome floated above the nave in a way Western builders wouldn't learn to copy for another two centuries. Into this church the Crusaders came. They hacked apart the silver altar screen and broke the gold altar itself into pieces small enough to carry. They led pack mules into the nave to haul the loot out. The animals slipped on the marble floors and left streaks of their dung. A Crusader prostitute, by the same account, was set on the throne of the patriarch, the head of the Orthodox Church. She was made to sing and dance for the soldiers while the looting went on around her. The chronicler, in the pages he later wrote, didn't pretend to find words equal to what he had witnessed; he simply listed it.

For nine hundred years, four great bronze horses had stood above the entrance of the Hippodrome. This was the chariot-racing stadium at the heart of the city, where the emperors had watched the games. The Crusaders took the horses down and shipped them to

Venice. They had once been gilded, and some of the gold leaf still clung to them. They were set up above the entrance of the Basilica of San Marco in Venice, where they stand today.

The Latin Empire of Constantinople was set up on May 16, 1204. The Crusade's own commander was passed over for the throne. The crown went instead to a Flemish count, who was crowned in the Hagia Sophia. Venice took for itself a quarter of the city. It also took the richest trade routes of the Byzantine Empire — the island of Crete and many in the Aegean, the harbors of the Greek coast and the Black Sea. Dandolo died in Constantinople a year later, in his nineties. He was buried in the Hagia Sophia itself, and his marker can still be seen there.

The Latin Empire lasted fifty-seven years. In 1261, the Byzantines took Constantinople back — but the empire they brought back was a shadow of what had stood there before. The libraries had been stripped, the treasuries emptied, the trade routes taken over by Venice. The Byzantium that limped on for the next two hundred years could no longer raise the armies that had once guarded southeastern Europe.

In 1453, the Ottomans took Constantinople. They used new bronze cannons that battered down the great

Theodosian walls. They renamed the city Istanbul and made it the seat of an empire. That empire would push as far west as Vienna and as far north as the Volga before it stopped. The fall of Constantinople in 1453 is usually taught as the end of the Middle Ages and the start of the modern world. One thing is rarely mentioned. The Christian city that fell in 1453 had been crippled, two and a half centuries earlier, by a debt the Fourth Crusade couldn't pay.

The split between the Catholic West and the Orthodox East had been made formal in 1054. At the time, the church quarrels behind it could still have been healed. In 1204 the split became permanent. Greek-speaking Christians didn't forget the prostitute on the patriarch's throne, or the mules in the nave of the Hagia Sophia. They didn't forget the relics carted off to Western cathedrals, where they're still shown as the spoils of war. The Orthodox Church and the Catholic Church stayed, and stay, apart.

In 2001, almost eight hundred years after the sack, Pope John Paul II met with the Orthodox Patriarch in Athens and formally apologized. Some memories, he said, are very painful. The Patriarch accepted the apology. The two churches stayed apart.

The bronze horses still stand above the front of St. Mark's Basilica in Venice. They're copies now. The originals were moved indoors in the 1980s to protect them from pollution. But the real horses are still there, in a small museum above the church, where you can stand close enough to touch them. They're the most costly horses in the world. They were the price of a fleet that couldn't be paid for, and a Crusade that turned into a sack, and an empire that never recovered, and a Church that hasn't been put back together.

Gold didn't cause the Fourth Crusade. Gold ended it. The men who sailed for Jerusalem in 1202 fell short of what they owed, and the rest of history rolled out of that shortfall — Constantinople sacked, Byzantium broken, Christianity split, Istanbul born. It all turned on one thing: no one in Venice was willing to forgive a debt.

Cairo, July 1324.

A hundred and twenty years after Constantinople burned, the dust on the western horizon belonged to an empire no Cairene had ever seen.

CHAPTER FOUR — THE PILGRIM WHO CRASHED AN ECONOMY

Generosity at the scale of empires has its costs. The largest of them are paid by people who never received any of it.

West Africa, Cairo, and Mecca, 1324–1325

The Cairo gatekeeper at the western edge of the city saw it first. Just after dawn on a hot day in July of 1324, the horizon to the southwest began to move. He climbed the parapet to look. Out of the dunes came what seemed, in the first uncertain light, to be a small army. As it drew closer, he saw that it wasn't an army at all but a caravan — the largest anyone in Cairo had ever seen come to the city walls. Thousands of men on foot, hundreds of camels, horsemen in cloaks, a front rank of slaves in silk. The dust raised by the marchers reached a hundred feet into the sky. The head of the column was already at the gate before its tail could be seen against the horizon.

At the center of the caravan rode a tall, lean man, sixty years old, in white robes and a gold-stitched turban. An honor guard of five hundred rode around him. He was the ninth ruler of the Mali Empire, and his name was Mansa Musa. He had come to perform the hajj, the holy trip every Muslim is expected to make to Mecca once in a lifetime. And he had chosen to make the journey in a way no one before him had ever tried.

He had brought enough gold with him to break the price of gold across the whole Mediterranean world for the next twelve years.

To understand how one man could do such a thing, you have to know where Mali had been for the last hundred years. And you have to know why no one in Cairo had quite grasped the size of it until they saw the dust on the horizon.

In 1324, the Mali Empire was the largest and richest state in Africa. It stretched from the Atlantic coast eastward across the grasslands for two thousand miles. From there it reached north into the southern Sahara and south into the rainforest belt. Its lands took in a swath of West Africa larger than Western Europe. And it controlled the great trans-Saharan trade routes. These carried gold north into the Islamic world, and salt, copper, and finished goods south into Africa. Inside its borders lay the gold-bearing regions of Bambuk and Bure, two of the richest gold fields known to the medieval world. By the most careful modern guesses, Mali at its peak made roughly half of all the gold moving through the Old World.

But Mali sat on the wrong side of the Sahara. Its gold flowed north, but its rulers didn't. The North African merchants who carried Malian gold dust to the markets of the Mediterranean coast had only the dimmest idea of where the gold came from. Somewhere beyond the desert, they knew, beyond the river the Arabs called the Nile of the Negroes — which we now call the Niger. In a country ruled by a Muslim king they had never seen. The Mediterranean world knew that Mali was rich. It didn't yet grasp how rich.

Mansa Musa was about to make it clear.

He had taken the throne of Mali around 1312, in his late forties. The mansa before him — most likely the last king, and possibly his cousin — had vanished trying to cross the Atlantic Ocean with a fleet of two thousand ships. (Whether that voyage really happened is argued by modern historians. The only source for it is Mansa Musa himself, telling the story to Egyptian chroniclers in Cairo.) Musa was handed a steady, wealthy, fast-growing empire, and he spent the first twelve years of his reign building it up. He pushed Mali's reach eastward into Songhai land and took the great trading city of Timbuktu under his direct rule. To his court he drew Islamic scholars, judges, builders, and poets from across the Muslim world.

He was a devout Muslim; the hajj wasn't a choice, and he meant to perform it. But he was also a king, and he knew that a king's journey is a king's statement. And he meant to make a statement the Islamic world wouldn't be able to forget.

The planning took years. He drew on his own treasury and on the output of the Bambuk and Bure gold fields. The numbers in the Arab chronicles are staggering. His caravan held sixty thousand people, twelve thousand of them personal slaves, who would each carry four pounds of gold bars on top of their other work. Eighty camels came too, each loaded with three hundred pounds of gold dust. Heralds, doctors, cooks — a small court on the move. He left his son to rule in his place and set out across the Sahara in 1324.

The desert crossing took eight months.

The caravan moved at the pace of a walking man and his animals — perhaps fifteen miles a day across the better stretches, less across the worst. It stopped often at oases to water and rest, and at each major stop Musa handed out gold. The local sheikhs who hosted him received some. So did the desert tribesmen who guided his guards through the hard passes. So did the camel-handlers, porters, and merchants who joined along the route. By the time he reached the southern edge of Egypt, his coming was already being told by every traveler who had crossed his path.

Cairo in 1324 was the largest city in the Mediterranean world. It held perhaps half a million people, ruled by the Mamluk Sultanate. This was a state founded by former slave-soldiers. They had seized the throne of Egypt in 1250 and were now the strongest Muslim power in the region. The sitting Sultan was a seasoned ruler in his third reign. He had been thrown out and brought back twice, and he wasn't used to being upstaged by visiting foreign kings.

Mansa Musa pitched his camp near the pyramids at Giza, outside the city walls, in July of 1324. He had no plan to leave for several months. He sent word of his arrival to the Sultan. The Sultan, following custom, sent gifts and asked him to visit the citadel.

Mansa Musa refused.

The problem was a matter of court manners. Mamluk rules required that any visiting ruler, on coming before the Sultan, kiss the ground at the Sultan's feet. It was a sign of bowing to the Sultan's power over all who came into his court. Mansa Musa had crossed an ocean of sand at the head of his own court, and he ruled an empire larger than Egypt itself. He thought this beneath him. For weeks, court messengers shuttled between the two camps. The Sultan wouldn't see Musa unless he kissed the ground. Musa wouldn't kiss the ground for any earthly king.

In the end a middle way was found. Musa was allowed to enter the court and bow before God rather than before the Sultan — a face-saving move that let both rulers feel they had won. When he came at last to the citadel, he came in grand style. He wore West African robes and a gold crown. His honor guard ringed him, criers walked ahead, and a train of slaves came behind carrying gifts. The gifts he brought to the Sultan himself came to fifty thousand gold dinars — a sum that stunned the Mamluk court.

And then the giving expanded outward.

For three months, Mansa Musa gave gold to everyone.

The four chief Islamic judges of Cairo, one for each school of law, were given gold, and so were the imams of the major mosques. Every government official and palace servant who came to call went away with some.

The merchants who supplied his camp charged him double, then triple, then ten times the going price. They sold him food, wine, cloth, weapons, perfume, and small treats, and he paid for all of it without haggling. When he walked through Cairo he handed gold to the beggars in the streets, and soon they followed him in such numbers that he couldn't leave his camp without being mobbed.

An Arab chronicler who talked to witnesses in Cairo twelve years later wrote that there was no person of note in the city — official, scholar, merchant, or noble — who went without. Each one received a robe of honor or a load of gold during those three months. He tried to figure out how much the caravan had given away. The lowest honest guess, he concluded, was beyond counting.

And then, slowly, the price of gold in Cairo began to fall.

The reason was simple. There was now far more gold in Cairo than three months before, yet the goods it could buy hadn't grown. Every merchant who had received gold from Musa wanted to spend it. Every merchant who hadn't was suddenly up against neighbors with three times their old cash. As they all bid for the same limited goods, prices climbed. And the value of gold, set against everything it could buy, fell.

By the time Mansa Musa left for Mecca in October of 1324, the gold dinar of Cairo had lost roughly a fifth of its value against goods. By the summer of 1325, when he finished the hajj and came back to Cairo on his way home, the loss was nearing one third. Long after he left, the market refused to recover. Twelve years later, when that same chronicler, al-Umari, sat down to write, he noted that the price of gold in Cairo had still not returned to what it had been before the pilgrim from Mali passed through.

The Mediterranean world had just lived through its first recorded inflation event caused by the spending of a single person.

The trip home is where the story turns from amazing to a little sad.

By 1325, Musa came back through Cairo on his way west. He had spent or given away a large share of the gold he had brought. He still had more than enough for the journey home. But the Mamluk merchants of Cairo, watching the price of gold keep falling in his wake, came to him with an offer. They would lend him gold, in any amount he wished, at a high rate of interest. He would pay it back once he reached Mali and could draw on the next year's mines. The terms were brutal. But Musa feared he would arrive home with too little to keep up the pride of his return, so he agreed. The merchants drained by his giving on the way out were made rich all over again by his debt on the way home.

It was the only big money mistake of his reign. He paid the debt in full within a year. But the picture of Mansa Musa borrowing back the gold he had given away himself is the one that stayed in the Arab chronicles. In a single deal, it shows how fully his visit had reshaped the money of the city he passed through.

He went on home across the Sahara. He had been gone two years.

He returned to Mali in 1325 not only with fame but with people. A poet and architect from Granada had joined the return caravan in Mecca and took up Musa's offer to come to Mali. In Timbuktu he designed the great Djinguereber Mosque — a mudbrick building with timber struts that still stands seven centuries later. A famous school grew up around it. By the fifteenth century it had made Timbuktu one of the leading homes of Islamic learning in Africa, its libraries holding, in time, hundreds of thousands of manuscripts.

For a generation after Mansa Musa's hajj, Mali was at its peak. The empire he handed to his son around 1337 stretched further, held more cities, hosted more scholars, and made more gold than any king before him had dreamed of.

He had also done something he didn't mean to do, and the results of it were just beginning.

He had put Mali on the maps of the people who had never been there.

In 1375, a Catalan Jewish mapmaker in Majorca made what's now called the Catalan Atlas — a richly drawn map of the known world, ordered for a royal court of Spain. In the southwest quadrant of the Old World, where earlier European maps had shown only vague desert, he drew the figure of a Black African king seated on a throne. He wore a gold crown. He held a gold ball as large as a melon. A caption beside him read, in medieval Catalan: This Negro lord is called Musse Melly, lord of the Negroes of Guinea. So plentiful is the gold found in his country that he's the richest and most noble king in all the land.

The Catalan Atlas passed among the courts of Europe. It was copied widely. The merchants of the

Mediterranean ports studied it closely. The Portuguese most of all took notice. In the early fifteenth century, with the backing of Prince Henry the Navigator, Portuguese ships began working their way steadily down the West African coast. They were looking for many things — fish, slaves, sugar islands, a sea route to India. But at the top of the list was the source of the gold the man on the Catalan Atlas had once given away.

By the 1480s the Portuguese had reached the Gulf of Guinea. They built a walled trading post — Saint George of the Mine — on the coast of what's now Ghana. Within a few decades, gold was flowing from West Africa to Lisbon by sea, in amounts that skipped the Saharan caravan routes for good. The trans-Saharan trade that had made Mali rich began to wither. The North African merchants who had carried Mali's gold north for centuries found their profits drying up. And the West African coast became, almost by chance, the staging ground for what would in the next century grow into the Atlantic slave trade.

By 1500, Mali was no longer the top power in West Africa. The Songhai Empire to its east had swallowed most of its land. By 1600, Mali was only a small kingdom around its first homeland on the upper Niger. By 1700, it was all but gone.

The man on the throne in the Catalan Atlas, holding up a piece of gold, had been dead for three and a half hundred years.

Mansa Musa had made no mistake. He had carried out a holy duty, in the manner of a king, and he had spent his own gold. He had built a mosque and a school and brought scholars to a city that had never had them before. Across the Islamic world, he had made his name stand for faith and giving. By any test he knew, he had done well.

But giving, on the scale he had done it, broke a market a thousand miles from home. And visibility, on the scale his caravan had earned him, painted his empire on a map for people who had been hungry to find it for a long time. The traders of Genoa didn't need to wait for an invitation. The Portuguese didn't need permission. And the maps outlived him by two hundred years, then five hundred, longer than the empire they had described.

The gold he gave away in Cairo slowly filtered through the markets and came to rest in the vaults and jewelry of the Mediterranean world. The gold still in the ground in Bambuk and Bure was harder for Mali to keep. The people who wanted it now knew exactly where it was.

Generosity broke an economy. Visibility broke an empire. Both took years to be felt. By the time anyone in Mali could see the harm, the men with caravels were already at the coast, asking where the gold came from.

Saxony, October 1517.

Two centuries after the maps had been drawn, another wagon rolled into another town, ringing another bell.

CHAPTER FIVE — THE FRIAR, THE COIN, AND THE COFFER

The gold that builds a great building can be the same gold that breaks the institution that builds it. The building gets finished anyway.

Saxony, Wittenberg, and Rome, 1515–1521

A wagon rolled into a German town square on an October afternoon in 1517 — a small wagon, drawn by two horses, the kind a country trader might use to carry turnips to market. But the load on this wagon was different. In the bed of it sat an iron-bound chest, big enough that two men were needed to lift it, locked with three locks and sealed across the top with the wax seal of the Pope. Beside the chest stood a Dominican friar in a black-and-white habit, ringing a small bell, and a crowd was already forming. He was used to the work by now; he had been doing this in towns across northern Germany for the better part of two years.

His name was Johann Tetzel. He was about fifty years old, a graduate of Leipzig, and a skilled preacher with the kind of carrying voice and flair for drama that brought peasants out of their houses to listen. He preached on one thing only: the saving of souls in purgatory.

When he had drawn a crowd, he would begin. In vivid and frightening words, he painted the suffering of the dead — the souls of mothers and fathers, husbands and wives, trapped in purgatory because of sins they hadn't fully confessed before they died. He would describe the cries of these souls, and tell the listeners that the dead were watching them now, begging for help. Then he would tell them that the help was at hand. The Pope himself, by his special power, had made it cheaper than ever before.

It was as simple as putting a coin in the chest.

His jingle, which Martin Luther would later quote in scorn, ran something like: As soon as the coin in the coffer rings, the soul from purgatory springs.

Peasants emptied their savings into the chest. Tetzel gave each giver a paper, an indulgence, stamped with the Pope's seal, promising that the named soul had been set free from purgatory. When the chest was full, it was loaded back onto the wagon, and the wagon rolled on to the next town. At the end of each trip, the gold was counted, weighed, and sent south, where it was split in two. Half of it went to Rome. The other half went to a counting house in Augsburg, owned by a banker named Jakob Fugger.

To see why a Dominican friar was driving a wagon full of peasants' coins across the German lands, you have to go back two years. The deal had been struck in a meeting in the Vatican.

The Pope was Leo X, a son of the Medici, the banking family that ruled Florence, raised to the papal throne in 1513 at the age of thirty-seven — the youngest pope in two hundred years. On the day he was chosen he's said to have told his brother: God has given us the papacy. Let us enjoy it. He was a polished, well-read, open-handed man, a friend to artists and a lover of good wine, and he was always short of money.

He had two very costly habits. The first was his own court, which staged feasts, hunts, plays, and parades on a scale that even the Italian nobles found over the top. The second was a building.

Back in 1506 the pope before him had decided that the old church of Saint Peter should be torn down and replaced. It had been built by the Emperor Constantine in the fourth century. Twelve hundred years old, it was plainly falling apart. He hired a master architect, ordered the old church pulled down, and laid the first stone of the largest cathedral the world had ever seen. The plan called for a dome larger than any in Rome and a hall longer than any in Europe. It would be filled with artwork by the best painters and carvers of the Italian Renaissance. By 1515 the bill was already growing past what any single pope could hope to raise. St. Peter's Basilica wouldn't be finished until 1626. By then twenty popes would have watched over its building.

Leo needed money, a great deal of it, and he needed it without end.

His method was indulgences. An indulgence was a piece of paper, signed by the Pope, that promised to shorten or wipe out a dead soul's time in purgatory. Purgatory was the cleansing fire that almost every Christian in those days believed they would have to pass through before reaching heaven. The Church had been selling these papers, in one form or another, for two hundred years. Scholars inside the Church had been uneasy about it for almost as long. Leo X, in 1515, set the unease aside and announced a new indulgence to pay for St. Peter's. A person could buy, for a gift sized to his means, the release of one named soul. The money would be gathered by chosen preachers and shipped to Rome.

The right to sell this indulgence across a stretch of the German lands went to a young Hohenzollern prince named Albrecht of Brandenburg.

Albrecht was twenty-five, and hungry for power in a way that bent the rules of Church law. He already held two German sees. Now he wanted Mainz as well — not only a great and wealthy see but one of the seven seats that chose the Holy Roman Emperor, the elected overlord of the German lands. Holding three sees at once was against Church law. Such a thing needed a special pardon from the Pope, and such pardons cost gold.

The Pope's office set the price for Albrecht's pardon at roughly twenty-one thousand gold ducats. Albrecht didn't have it. He went to the richest banker in Europe to borrow it.

In a paneled meeting room in Augsburg, in the spring of 1514, Jakob Fugger received the young archbishop. Fugger was then in his late fifties, a third-generation Augsburg trader. He had inherited a cloth business and built it, in his lifetime, into the most powerful bank in the German-speaking world. He had lent money to kings, emperors, and popes; to the Habsburgs he had lent the gold that bought Charles V

— the Habsburg heir who would rule Spain, Germany, and the Americas — the imperial crown a few years before. He held the silver and copper mines of central Europe as security. By some modern guesses he was the richest person in all of history, measured against the economy of his day.

He was also, for a man of his rank, deeply devout — a strict Catholic who had built poorhouses for the Augsburg poor and saw his banking as a Christian calling. He heard out the archbishop's request, weighed the security on offer, and named his terms.

The terms were simple. Fugger would advance the twenty-one thousand ducats, and Albrecht would receive his three sees. The loan would be paid back, with interest, out of the earnings of the new indulgence drive — the very drive the Pope was about to allow across Albrecht's German lands. The Pope quietly blessed it, and so the gold gathered from German peasants would be split in half. One share went to Rome, for St. Peter's, and the other to Fugger's counting house in Augsburg, to repay Albrecht's loan. Albrecht signed, Fugger sent the ducats, and the young archbishop went home to wait for the friars to arrive.

The friar Tetzel was the one chosen to do the actual collecting.

For two years, Tetzel and his fellow preachers worked the German lands. They moved from town to town with their chests and their seal and their bell. In market squares they preached. In churches they preached too, before priests who were sometimes uneasy and sometimes glad to help. They worked the small states along the Saxon border most of all, because that was Albrecht's land and the land of greatest gain.

The pattern, in any given Saxon or Brandenburg town that spring, ran something like this. A widow in her sixties — or a young father with a sick child, or a peasant who had buried his mother the year before — would come to the church on the day Tetzel was preaching. She would stand at the back. From the pulpit she would hear him tell of the dead souls trapped in purgatory, burning until the last of their sins was cleaned away. She would hear him say that the few silver pfennigs in her purse could lift a soul she loved out of that fire and into heaven. The Pope himself, by his holy power, swore it was so.

She would walk to the chest at the front of the church and empty her savings into it. In return she would be handed a paper, signed and sealed, naming the soul that had just been freed. She would walk home in the rain.

The campaign worked. The chests filled, the wagons rolled south, and the gold reached Augsburg and Rome on schedule. By the autumn of 1517 it had run long enough that the Fugger loan was on track to be repaid, and in Rome the St. Peter's work was plainly moving ahead. From Leo X's point of view, the deal was a full success.

A young Augustinian monk in the small university town of Wittenberg, in the next-door state of Saxony, was, however, paying attention.

Martin Luther was thirty-three years old, an Augustinian monk and university teacher in Wittenberg. For years he had wrestled, alone, with the question of whether God could ever be brought to forgive him. In his lectures on the Letter of Paul to the Romans, he had begun to think that being saved came not from anything a person did. It came not from penance, not from pilgrimage, not from a bought indulgence, but from faith alone. He was working out the argument quietly, in Latin, when Tetzel's wagons began crossing into the parishes around Wittenberg.

Saxon peasants who had bought indulgences from Tetzel came to Luther for confession. They expected that the paper settled the matter and that they need not be sorry for their sins at all. Luther was horrified. He saw his own people being told that God's forgiveness was for sale.

October 31, 1517, was the eve of All Saints' Day. On that day pilgrims would come to the church at Wittenberg and pay to view its collection of holy relics. On that day Luther wrote a letter to Archbishop Albrecht. With it he sent a list of ninety-five points, in Latin, on the subject of indulgences. The points were scholar's theses, meant to be argued at the university. They claimed, in calm and careful form, that the sale of indulgences was false teaching. They said the Pope had no power over souls in purgatory, and that a Christian who was truly sorry needed no bought paper. And they said that Pope Leo, if he knew what was being done in his name, would rather see St. Peter's burned to the ground than built from the savings of the poor.

By tradition, Luther also nailed the theses to the door of the Castle Church at Wittenberg. Whether he truly did this is argued over by historians; the date and the letter aren't.

He hadn't meant to start a revolution. He had meant to start a scholar's debate.

What happened instead came down to the new German printing presses. They had been invented less than seventy years before, in Mainz, by Gutenberg, and by now they stood in every big city in central Europe. The presses picked up the theses, turned them from Latin into German, and printed them in numbers no scholar's paper had ever reached. Within two weeks the theses were being read across Germany. Within two months they were in Rome, in France, in England. By Christmas of 1517, Luther was a famous man whether he wished to be or not.

Tetzel, ordered by his leaders to answer, preached against Luther. Luther answered in print. The Dominican order turned against Luther; the Augustinian order quietly backed him. The Pope, annoyed by what he first took for a squabble between monks, asked Luther's leaders to silence him. They tried. Luther refused to be silenced.

For three years he refused to take back a word. Called before the Pope's men and told to recant, he didn't. Set against leading Catholic scholars in debate, he wouldn't back down. And he kept publishing — writings that went far past indulgences to attack the whole shape of the papal Church, the meaning of the sacraments, the very claim that priests alone could stand between God and a believer.

In January of 1521, Pope Leo X formally cast him out of the Church. Rome was done with him. That

April the new Holy Roman Emperor summoned Luther to appear before the Imperial Diet in the city of Worms — Charles V, twenty years old, ruler of Spain, Germany, and a vast stretch of the Americas.

Luther arrived at Worms on April 16, 1521, guarded by German knights who took his side, expecting to be killed. The last heretic called to such a hearing, Jan Hus, had been burned in spite of a promise of safe passage.

He was led into the great hall before the Emperor and a roomful of princes, bishops, and lawyers. His books were stacked on a table. Twice he was asked whether he would take back what they said. He asked for a day to think. The next afternoon, April 18, he gave his answer.

He said that he couldn't take back anything unless he was shown, by Scripture or by plain reason, that he was wrong. To go against his conscience, he said, was neither right nor safe. Then the words that outlived him: Here I stand. I can do no other. God help me. Amen.

The Emperor wasn't moved by any of it. The Edict of Worms, handed down in May, declared Luther an outlaw whom any subject of the Empire could lawfully kill on sight.

On Luther's way home from Worms, a band of armed men stopped his wagon in a forest and carried him off. The men were soldiers of Frederick the Wise of Saxony, who had decided to protect his unruly monk. They took Luther to Wartburg Castle, a fort on a wooded hilltop, and kept him there for ten months under a false name and a long beard. While in hiding he turned the New Testament from Greek into German. That work would shape the German language itself for the next four hundred years. It also put the Bible, for the first time, into the hands of any German who could read and afford a printed book.

What followed in central Europe over the next hundred years was the slow, unstoppable breaking apart of Western Christianity.

Lutheranism spread through the German states, the Nordic kingdoms, the Netherlands, and the British Isles. The princes who took it up seized the lands and incomes of the Catholic monasteries for themselves. By 1555 the Holy Roman Empire was so split that a treaty had to be signed at Augsburg. It gave each German prince the right to choose Catholicism or Lutheranism for his own land.

The deal didn't hold. In 1618, religious war broke out between the Catholic and Protestant princes of central Europe — what we now call the Thirty Years' War. It drew in most of the great powers around them. By the time the war ended in 1648, perhaps eight million people had died in the German-speaking lands alone. That was a larger share of central Europe's people than would die in either World War.

In Rome, the long work on St. Peter's went on. Pope Leo X died in 1521 — the year of Luther's stand at Worms — leaving the basilica half-built. It would take another hundred years, twenty popes, and Michelangelo's dome to finish it. The church was blessed and opened in November of 1626.

By that time, more than half of Europe had left the Catholic Church.

Pope Leo X had needed gold for a building. He had hired a friar with a wagon to collect it from German peasants, and the friar had collected it well and on schedule. The gold had flowed to Rome and to Augsburg, the bank had been paid, the building had risen, and the whole system had worked just the way Leo meant it to.

It had also, along the way, lit a fire in the spiritual conscience of a monk three hundred miles off who could no longer bear to watch the gold go by. And so the Reformation began in a wagon — a wagon carrying coins paid by people who had been told the coins would shorten their dead parents' time in purgatory. Those coins reached the building.

The gold paid for the dome. The dome paid for the Reformation. By the time the dome was finished, the Church it had been built to honor had been broken in half.

Cajamarca, November 1532.

Fifteen years after Luther's letter, Spanish hulls had been crossing the Atlantic for a generation.

CHAPTER SIX — A ROOM FULL OF GOLD AND A MAN THEY KILLED ANYWAY

A deal is worth what the stronger side chooses to keep of it. The largest ransom ever paid was paid in full.

Cajamarca, Peru, November 1532 – July 1533

Atahualpa entered the plaza at Cajamarca in the late afternoon of November 16, 1532, riding a golden litter carried by eighty lords in blue cloaks. The Inca emperor was about thirty years old. He wore a crown of white feathers above a heavy gold collar set with green stones, and ahead of him servants swept the road with palm fronds. His royal guard walked beside him carrying no weapons, since this was a peace meeting and his eighty thousand troops were camped outside the city. The plaza was empty.

He had been told there were strangers in the city, fewer than two hundred of them. They had shown up on the coast a few months back and had asked, in kind words, for a meeting. He was here to see them.

The strangers were one hundred and sixty-eight Spaniards, hidden in the covered walkways around the square. They had four small cannon and twelve harquebuses, the early Spanish guns with their slow matchlock fuses, and sixty-two horses, animals the Inca world had never once seen. Their leader was a man named Francisco Pizarro, a Spanish soldier in his fifties who couldn't read. He had spent the last thirty years in the New World, waiting for a day like this one.

By the time the sun set, thousands of Inca would be dead in the plaza, Atahualpa would be a prisoner, and the largest empire in the New World would have begun to come apart in his absence.

The conquest of Peru began with a disease.

In 1527, somewhere on the northern edge of the Inca Empire — in the area around modern Quito, Ecuador — the ruling Inca emperor Huayna Capac fell suddenly ill. His court and his chosen heir fell ill too, and within days they were dead. The disease was almost certainly smallpox. The Inca had no defense against it. It had jumped from the Spanish towns in Panama and moved faster than any Spanish soldier, ahead of the first contact between Europeans and the Inca state.

His death left the empire with no clear heir. Two of his sons each claimed the throne. Huascar held the capital city of Cuzco, in the south. Atahualpa held

Quito, in the north, along with the army that had served their father. A four-year civil war followed. By the spring of 1532, Atahualpa's generals had beaten Huascar's army outside Cuzco and taken him alive. Atahualpa was now moving slowly south to claim the capital, his veteran army with him. He was at the royal hot springs outside Cajamarca, resting from the war, when word reached him that strangers had landed on the coast.

He wasn't much worried. They were one hundred and sixty-eight men. He had eighty thousand.

The strangers had been moving inland for two months. They were the third Spanish band to try to reach into the Andes. The two before them had ended in starvation and retreat. Their leader, Francisco Pizarro, was a distant cousin of Hernan Cortes. Cortes had taken the Aztec Empire of Mexico ten years earlier with a small band of men much like this one. Pizarro had spent his life chasing the rumor that something just as rich lay south of Panama. For years he had heard the stories of a wealthy mountain kingdom, and in 1529 he had gone back to Spain and talked the Emperor Charles V into giving him the legal right to take it.

He had brought his four brothers with him. With them came a Dominican friar named Valverde, there to handle the church excuses that Spanish conquest called for, and one of Cortes's battle-hardened horse captains, Hernando de Soto, who would later lead his own march through what's now the American Southeast. They had landed on the Peruvian coast in early 1532, founded a small settlement, and begun the long march east into the Andes.

Pizarro reached Cajamarca on November 15, 1532. The city was empty; its people had been moved out to give the Inca army room to fight. From the heights above the city he could see the smoke of Atahualpa's camp in the hills — tens of thousands of tents, an army that outnumbered his force four hundred to one. His men were terrified. Pizarro, his nerve intact, sent de Soto and a small group to the Inca camp with a polite invitation. Would the great king do the Spanish captain the honor of visiting the strangers in the city the next day?

Atahualpa agreed.

That night, Pizarro set his men in the covered walkways around the plaza. He hid the cavalry in the buildings on the long sides. He placed the cannons and harquebuses in the upper rooms, with a clear line of fire onto the open square. He gave his orders: no one was to move until the signal came. The signal would be the firing of the first cannon.

The Inca came in slowly the next afternoon. The long line took hours to gather outside the city and march in. Atahualpa was carried into the empty plaza on his golden litter. Perhaps five thousand of his followers crowded in behind him, most of them unarmed dancers, singers, and sweepers. A smaller number were bodyguards carrying small ritual axes. The Spanish soldiers, watching from their hidden spots, were sweating hard despite the cold mountain air. Some of them, by their own later accounts, lost control of their bowels.

Pizarro sent Friar Valverde into the plaza to meet the emperor.

Valverde came up to the golden litter holding a breviary — a small leather-bound book of Catholic prayers. Through a young Inca translator, he made the formal Spanish demand. The king was to accept Jesus Christ as God. He was to accept the Pope in Rome as God's voice on earth, and the Emperor Charles V as God's chosen ruler over the lands of the Americas. The translator did his best with ideas that didn't exist in his language. Atahualpa, who had never seen a book before, asked to look at it. Valverde handed it over. The king held the breviary to his ear, listened, heard nothing, and dropped it on the ground.

Valverde turned and called out to Pizarro, in Spanish, that the king had thrown down the holy book. Pizarro gave the signal. The first cannon fired.

What happened next took less than two hours.

The cavalry burst out of the side walkways into the tightly packed Inca crowd, and the horses — animals Atahualpa's people had never seen — threw them into panic. From the upper rooms the guns fired down into the square, and the Spanish foot soldiers charged with swords. They cut down the unarmed Inca, who had no weapon that could pierce Spanish steel armor and had never faced horsemen in a fight.

The eighty nobles who carried the litter held it up even as their hands were cut off. They took each other's place as they fell, refusing to let the king touch the ground. When the last of them was killed, Pizarro himself reached the litter, fought through the few guards left, and pulled Atahualpa down. The Spanish captain took a cut on the hand from one of his own men in the chaos — the only Spanish wound of the day.

By the time the sun set, two to seven thousand Inca — the count varies by source — lay dead in the plaza and in the streets nearby. The Spanish hadn't lost a single man. Atahualpa was taken to a house at the edge of the plaza and locked in.

He realized within days what the strangers had come for.

The Spanish had been moving through the city, stripping it of every gold ornament they could find. The Inca used gold mostly to decorate temples, not as money. So it was everywhere — on the walls, the cups, the doorframes, the small statues in the niches. Atahualpa watched this closely. He saw, in a way Pizarro perhaps didn't grasp at first, what it all meant. The strangers didn't want the empire. They wanted the metal.

He made an offer.

He would fill the very room he was held in with gold ornaments, melted down and recast where needed. By the best counts the room was twenty-two feet long and seventeen feet wide. The ceiling stood about nine feet high. He drew a line on the wall, his hand stretched as high as he could reach — roughly eight feet — and the gold would rise to that mark. He would also fill two smaller rooms next door with silver, to the same height, twice over. In exchange he would be set free.

Pizarro agreed. The deal was put in writing, witnessed by a notary, and dated. Inca runners were sent across the empire with the king's orders. Every temple, every palace, every shrine was to be stripped of its gold. The gold would be carried to Cajamarca and handed to the strangers.

It took eight months.

The Inca Empire reached from the northern edge in modern Ecuador to the southern edge in northern Chile. That span was larger than the United States east of the Mississippi. Across all of it, runners carried the king's orders out and gold-laden caravans came back. The runners moved along the royal roads. These were thousands of miles of stone-paved highway that climbed across the Andes in stairs and switchbacks. The roads hung over gorges on woven-fiber rope bridges, and relay teams tied the land together. A team of runners could carry a message from Quito to Cuzco in seven days. The same roads now carried the gold the other way.

Llama trains came down out of the high passes, each animal loaded with as much as it could bear. The famous gold panels of the Temple of the Sun at Cuzco had once covered the inner walls of the holiest building in the empire. They were hammered out in thin sheets that showed the rays of the sun. Now priests under guard pried them loose and packed them for the journey north.

Statues of past emperors. Golden plants and animals from the sacred gardens at the temple. There, every species in the Inca world had been copied in life-sized gold and silver, leaf by leaf and stem by stem. Sacred cups older than memory. Funeral masks taken from the dried bodies of past rulers. Their bodies had been kept in their palaces, with their gold intact, for hundreds of years after they died.

On the orders of the captive king, every royal city in the Andes was stripped clean. His own priests and officials did it. They obeyed as they would have obeyed any other royal command. And they watched a thousand years of holy and royal art get packed onto the backs of llamas and walked north to the Spanish camp.

The Spanish set up melting furnaces. The gold ornaments had taken Inca craftsmen centuries to make, and they held the whole religious heritage of the empire. Now they were broken into pieces. They were melted into plain, standard bars that could be weighed, taxed, and split up. Almost nothing of the original work survived. A few small pieces escaped the furnaces.

They were too lovely for some Spaniards to give up, and these later made their way to European collections.

The room filled. By June of 1533 the line on the wall was reached. The notary wrote down the totals: roughly 13,400 pounds of gold and 26,000 pounds of silver. At modern prices the gold alone would be worth more than three hundred million dollars. In sixteenth-century Spain, where most workers earned a few coins a day, no single deal in the country's history had ever come close to such a sum.

The Inca had fulfilled the contract.

The Spanish called a trial.

The excuse was Pizarro's longtime partner in the conquest, who had arrived in April 1533 with two hundred fresh Spanish soldiers and a firm demand that he and his men share in the ransom. Those new men changed the politics of the camp. As long as Atahualpa was the prisoner of the original 168, those 168 could expect to keep his ransom for themselves. Now another two hundred Spaniards were claiming a share. The math no longer worked. And Atahualpa, once freed, would surely have some feelings about the men who had butchered his court and held him captive for eight months. He was also, the Spanish told themselves, secretly ordering an Inca army to march on Cajamarca and free him.

So Pizarro called together a court of Spanish soldiers — a body with no legal power over an Inca emperor under any law there was. They charged Atahualpa with treason against Spain, a country he had never heard of until November. They charged him with idolatry, the worship of the Inca sun god rather than the Christian one. They charged him with polygamy. And they charged him with the murder of his half-brother Huascar. Huascar had in fact been killed earlier that year, on Atahualpa's orders, during the civil war.

The verdict was guilty. The sentence was burning at the stake.

On July 26, 1533, Atahualpa was led into the plaza at Cajamarca — the same plaza where he had been captured eight months earlier — to be burned. Friar Valverde came to him with a final choice. If he would accept Christian baptism, his sentence would be changed from burning, which the Inca believed blocked the soul's journey after death, to strangling by garrote. Atahualpa agreed. He was baptized, given the Christian name Francisco — after Pizarro himself — and then garroted in the square. He was buried as a Christian.

The Spanish marched south to Cuzco, took the royal capital without a real fight, and set up a puppet emperor of their own choosing. By 1572, after forty years of on-and-off rebellion, the last Inca heir had been put to death. The empire that had ruled the western half of South America for more than a century was gone. It lived on only as a memory, and as a people of converted laborers in Spanish silver mines.

The gold of Cajamarca was the beginning, not the end, of what the Spanish would take out of the Andes. The story of a room filled to the ceiling with real gold fed a European dream of El Dorado, a golden king ruling a city of gold somewhere in the unmapped interior. That myth would drive a century of doomed expeditions into the Amazon, most of them ending in starvation and fever, all of them chasing a second Cajamarca that wasn't there.

The ransom was split among the Spaniards there and shipped to Spain. A fifth, the King's share, went to Charles V. The captains and cavalry took the largest portions, the foot soldiers smaller ones. Each of Pizarro's original 168 got a fortune. Some wasted it. Some bought estates and titles and vanished into the Spanish nobility. But the ransom, huge as it was, was only the surface gold of the Inca world: the temple panels and royal jewels that could be quickly stripped and weighed.

Under the surface lay the mines. The Inca had mined gold and silver in the Andes for hundreds of years. But they did it on a small scale, for ornament and ritual, not for trade. Starting in the 1540s, the Spanish would find the silver mountain at Potosi and the gold fields beyond it. Over the next three centuries they would pull from them a flood of precious metal. It was enough to reshape the European economy, the world economy, and the life of every laborer in the Andes who could be forced to dig it. That story belongs to the next chapter.

What the ransom room itself bought was something more exact. It bought Pizarro the conquest of Peru. It bought the Spanish crown the largest single transfer of wealth it had ever received. And it gave the world a lesson in what could be taken from a New World ruler in exchange for nothing.

The room still stands in Cajamarca. It's built of squared stone, with thick walls and a single small window, on a quiet street a few blocks from the modern cathedral. The Spanish never tore it down. A red line is painted on one wall at the height Atahualpa had marked with his stretched-out arm — about eight feet, the reach of a tall man. Tourists come through. They touch the wall. They take photographs.

The largest ransom in human history was paid in full. The man who paid it died anyway. The empire that paid it ended within a generation. And the room is small enough, in person, that a visitor standing inside it can take it all in without turning his head.

The true instrument of conquest hadn't been the steel of the Spanish swords. It hadn't been the powder of the guns, or the smallpox that killed the old emperor, or even the long civil war the smallpox had set off. It was the deal written down in November of 1532 and witnessed by a Spanish notary: a contract for a load of gold in exchange for the life of a man.

The Inca delivered. The Spanish didn't. The man was killed, the gold was taken, the empire was swallowed, and the room remained.

Cerro Rico, April 1545.

Twelve years after the room at Cajamarca, a herder's fire was burning above an empty mountain.

CHAPTER SEVEN — SPAIN DROWNS EUROPE IN AMERICAN SILVER

It's possible to own the world's largest source of wealth and to be poorer for it. It's even possible to die of it.

Potosi, Upper Peru, 1545–1650

In April of 1545, a llama herder named Diego Huallpa was working high on the side of a cone-shaped mountain in what's today southern Bolivia. One of his animals broke loose and ran up the slope, and he climbed after it over steep, cold ground. He was at thirteen and a half thousand feet, up in the thin air of the central Andes, where even the grass that grew was sparse and tough. By the time he caught up with the llama, the sun was setting. He chose to spend the night where he was rather than go down in the dark.

He gathered what dry shrub he could find and lit a fire against the cold. He slept beside it.

When he woke at dawn, he saw something he didn't expect. A thin silver ribbon had formed in the cooled ash where the fire had been. It had melted out of the rock he had built the fire on. The mountain itself, it seemed, was made of silver.

He carried a piece of it down. Within weeks, the secret was out. Within months, Spanish miners were swarming the slope. By the end of 1545, the Spanish crown had logged the find. At the foot of the mountain it founded a town called the Villa Imperial de Potosi.

That town would, within seventy years, become one of the largest cities in the world. The mountain would, within three centuries, give up more than half of all the silver mined on earth. The silver would, within a lifetime, reshape the economy of Europe, China, India, and the Ottoman Empire. And the workers who dug it out would die in numbers no one bothered to count with care — somewhere between four and eight million of them, over the three hundred years the mountain was worked.

The silver was, in the plainest sense, the foundation the first global economy stood upon.

It also bankrupted the country that owned the mountain.

Cerro Rico — the Rich Hill — sits in what was, in 1545, the southern edge of Spain's newly conquered Andean land. The conquest of the Inca had been finished only a decade before. The puppet emperors set up by the Pizarro brothers still faced the odd uprising.

But the surface silver of the old Inca empire had mostly been seized and shipped to Spain. The ore that was left lay scattered, and the Spanish didn't yet know where the next great strike would come from.

Cerro Rico answered the question.

The Inca had known about Cerro Rico. For centuries, local Indigenous miners had taken small amounts of silver out of it. They used little fires to roast the ore and simple furnaces to draw out the metal. One Spanish story holds that the Inca emperor himself once tried to start real mining on Cerro Rico. A voice from the mountain is said to have warned him off: the silver here isn't for you; it's for those who come later. Spanish writers almost certainly made the tale up later, to excuse the conquest. But the point underneath it was true. The Inca had treated Cerro Rico as a small source, not as the base of an empire.

The Spanish had no such restraint.

By 1550, five years after the herder's fire, perhaps twenty thousand people were living and working on the slopes of the mountain. By 1572, the Spanish viceroy in Lima would make Potosi the engine of the Spanish economy. A hard-headed official named Francisco de Toledo, he had been sent from Madrid for one job: to organize the empire's income.

Toledo's tool was a labor system called the mita.

He had taken the name from an Inca custom. The Inca had asked each village in the empire for a turn of labor — a few weeks each year, owed to the state, spent on roads, terraces, or temples. Toledo took the word and the shape of it and bent them to a new use. The zone ran about three hundred miles around Potosi. Under the Spanish mita, every Indigenous male in it aged eighteen to fifty had to serve in turn. Each owed a full year in the silver mines. One out of every seven grown men in the zone was called up each year. The drafted worker — the mitayo — was paid a token wage. He brought his wife and children with him when he could. The Spanish liked whole families to come. They didn't want the workers slipping away in the night.

By 1610, about one hundred and sixty thousand people lived in Potosi — more than London, more than Venice, more than Madrid or Paris in the same decade. By head count, it was one of the four or five largest cities in the world.

It was also the highest. At thirteen and a half thousand feet, the air held about sixty percent of the oxygen of sea level. The winters fell far below freezing.

The soil grew almost nothing, and water and firewood had to be carried in. Every potato eaten in Potosi came over the mountains on the back of a llama or an Indigenous porter. Every loaf of bread came from grain grown a hundred miles away. Wine for the city's taverns came from the coast of Peru, then over two ranges of the Andes by mule. The city stood only because of the silver.

The work inside the mountain killed people steadily.

The mitayos went into the tunnels at dawn on Mondays, carrying a week's worth of food in a leather pouch. They didn't come out again until Saturday. They worked by candlelight, in shifts of twelve hours, in tunnels that pinched tighter as they sank deeper into Cerro Rico. The air was poison: rock dust, the smoke of mercury furnaces, the breath of the men around them. They drilled the rock with iron tools and broke it loose with their hands. They hauled the ore up ladders of leather and timber that ran for hundreds of feet. At the top of the shaft they handed it over to the men who treated it. Then they went back down for another load.

A Spanish miner had worked out a new method in Mexico in the 1550s. It pulled silver from low-grade ore using mercury — the so-called patio process. Crushed ore was mixed with mercury in shallow open yards, the patios. There the mercury bonded with the silver, and heat could then split them apart. The method was far faster than the old smelting. It made it possible to work the thin veins of Cerro Rico that hadn't paid before. It was also catastrophic for the workers who handled it. Mercury vapor poisons the nerves; mercury that pools on skin soaks straight through it; mercury in the groundwater taints everything that drinks it. For as long as the patio process went on, the rivers below Potosi ran milky with mercury for miles below the refining yards, at levels that would shut them down today.

The mercury itself came from another mine. This was the Huancavelica mountain in central Peru, which the Spanish also worked with drafted Indigenous labor. Huancavelica's miners died even faster than Potosi's. The mercury they dug out was carried by mule train across thousands of miles of the Andes to Potosi. There it was used to kill the men digging out the silver. The two mountains were paired in death and in revenue, and between them they were the engine of the Spanish colonial economy in South America.

Death tolls from the centuries of work are hard to pin down, because no one was counting with care. Modern guesses of how many mitayos died in Potosi over three hundred years run from four million to eight million. The number is unsure; the scale isn't.

It's worth slowing, once, on a single one of them. A man went up the same leather-and-timber ladder he had climbed every dawn that week. This time other men carried him. At the top there was the cold and the thin light and the mountain going on as before. The ore he had cut loose with his hands went into the furnaces below, where the mercury drew the silver out of it. The silver went on to the mint, and then into a coin, and then onto a mule, and then across two oceans into the wider money of the world, where some of it still circulates. The man stayed on the mountain. No one wrote down his name, because names weren't the thing being counted. What was being counted was the silver, and the silver was the only part of him that left.

What the silver produced, in the wider world, was the first global economy. Diego Huallpa had climbed that cold slope after a loose llama. What he started that night — fire on rock, a thin ribbon of silver in the ash — was still running, a century later, across three oceans.

The Spanish struck the silver at Potosi into coins — the peso de a ocho, the piece of eight. Each coin held roughly an ounce of silver and was stamped with the Habsburg arms. Mule trains carried these coins across the Andes to the coast, and ships took them north to join the so-called Treasure Fleets that sailed each year across the Caribbean and the Atlantic to Spain. From Spain, the silver went where the demand was — and the demand was nearly everywhere.

A share stayed in Spain itself, where it paid for the wars of the Habsburg kings. There were the wars against the Dutch Revolt and against the Ottoman Empire in the Mediterranean. There were the wars against the French, the English, and the Protestants of Germany. Spain in the late sixteenth and seventeenth centuries was almost always at war on three or four fronts. The wars were paid for in silver.

A larger share flowed across Europe to clear Spanish debts with the bankers of Genoa and the other great money centers. They had lent the Spanish crown money against the next Treasure Fleet. The silver that reached Seville often didn't stay in Seville long. Foreign lenders claimed it before Spain could spend it. The Genoese above all became, in the late sixteenth century, the real bankers of the Spanish Empire. The silver of Potosi made Italian merchant houses far richer than it made the Spanish state.

And a very large share — by some guesses a full third of all the silver Potosi made — flowed east to Asia.

In 1571, the Spanish founded Manila in the Philippines. They opened what would become the longest steady trade route in human history before the steamship: the Manila Galleon. Each year, a Spanish galleon left the port of Acapulco on the Pacific coast of Mexico. It was loaded with silver pesos struck in Potosi, and it crossed the Pacific to Manila. There the silver was traded for Chinese silks, porcelain, jade, spices, and tea. Chinese junks brought these goods to Manila from the southern Chinese coast. The galleon then sailed back to Acapulco. The cargo crossed Mexico by mule to the Atlantic coast, and the goods reached Europe by way of Spain.

China was the biggest market, and there was a reason. In 1581 the Ming dynasty reformed its tax system — the so-called Single Whip Reform — so that taxes now had to be paid in silver rather than in goods or labor. Almost overnight, that created a Chinese hunger for silver China's own mines couldn't feed. The price followed. Silver fetched far more in China than in Europe, so when Spanish merchants bought silk in Manila with Potosi silver, they were really playing the gap between the two markets. The silver flowed east;

the goods flowed west; the gap closed slowly over a century and a half.

The Manila Galleon ran without a break from 1565 to 1815 — two hundred and fifty years. It was the first regular link across the Pacific in human history, and it ran on Potosi silver. The Chinese silk trade, the porcelain trade that flooded European markets, the long Asian tie the Spanish Empire held from a single Pacific port — all of it was paid for by the drafted mitayos digging in the Andean cold.

While the galleons loaded in Acapulco, the men who made the silver possible were still underground. Still Monday through Saturday. Still hauling ore up the leather ladders in the dark.

What this looked like, at ground level, was something most of the people living through it couldn't name.

Picture a journeyman wool-comber in a Castilian town like Cuenca. In 1565 he might have earned twelve maravedis a day, the same daily wage his father had earned in 1545. Ten years later, in 1575, he earned the same twelve maravedis. The coin bore the same king's face. The same Castilian mint made it. But the loaf of bread that had cost him four maravedis in 1565 now cost him seven. His wife had given up buying meat. His rent had risen twice.

His boss hadn't raised his wage. The finished wool cloth he combed, the boss told him, sold for not much more than it had ten years back. The wool-comber couldn't have said what was happening to his money. No one in his town could have said it. He might have turned the maravedi over in his fingers on the way home — same weight, same stamp, same cold edge. The coin felt the same in his hand. The bread was the same bread. The world around the coin had quietly become a different world.

What had changed was the silver flowing into Spain from across the Atlantic — silver cut from Cerro Rico by a hundred thousand drafted men who had no choice in the matter. The flood of American silver into Europe began in the 1540s and ran for over a century. It caused what historians now call the Price Revolution. From roughly 1500 to 1650, the price of ordinary goods in most of Europe roughly tripled. It was the same engine that had worked in Cairo in 1325, when Mansa Musa's gold crashed the dinar — only now across a whole continent and over a longer span.

The logic was simple. More silver in use meant each piece of silver was worth less. Landowners who could raise rents came out ahead; wage workers who couldn't raise wages didn't. Year by year, the journeymen of Cuenca and a thousand other towns grew poorer than their fathers had been. They never quite knew why. The old late-medieval order had favored small farmers and skilled craftsmen, and the silver flood bent it into a new shape — one that favored money over work.

Modern historians still argue over exactly how much American silver drove the Price Revolution. There were other causes too — a growing population, the cheapening of coins. But on one point they agree: without the silver, the rise wouldn't have reached the scale it did. And what that rise did, in the end, was move wealth in one direction. It flowed away from people who worked for wages. It flowed toward people who owned land, who held the loan papers behind the wars of the Spanish kings, who could simply raise their prices faster than their costs.

The strangest twist of the silver flood showed up in the country that, on paper, owned the mountain.

Spain went bankrupt.

It went bankrupt again and again. The Spanish crown formally defaulted on its debts in 1557, again in 1560, again in 1575, again in 1596, again in 1607, again in 1627, again in 1647, and again in 1652. Eight state bankruptcies in less than a century. The country that made more silver than any other on earth couldn't, somehow, keep itself out of the red. While the crown's bankers quarreled over the defaulted bonds in Seville, the mitayo's family was still camped on the mountain's lower slope, waiting for Monday.

The reasons were built in. Spain spent the silver as fast as it came, on wars and on goods Spain itself didn't make. The Spanish economy had almost nothing of its own to sell. Its farms were run poorly. Cheaper Dutch and English goods beat its workshops. Its wool was sold raw to foreign weavers, and its ships were mostly built by foreign hands. The silver came in and went out the next week. When the next Treasure Fleet was late, the Spanish state couldn't pay its soldiers, its sailors, or its lenders.

By 1700, the country that had launched the global silver economy was a second-rate power in Europe. The Habsburg line that had ruled Spain since 1516 died out with the childless Charles II. In his will he left the Spanish throne to a French Bourbon prince — and that set off the War of Spanish Succession, which redrew the map of Europe. Spain itself, the mountain still tied to it through colonial rule, no longer counted at the top European tables.

The mountain kept giving. It was worked through the eighteenth century, more slowly through the nineteenth, on and off through the twentieth. Even today, in the twenty-first century, miners are still digging into the side of Cerro Rico. Not for silver now — most of the rich ore is gone — but for tin and zinc, in cooperatives that work at the edges of the law and of safety. Little has changed underground. The miners use the same shovels and the same wooden ladders their ancestors used four hundred years ago, and chew the same coca leaves to dull hunger and altitude sickness.

They die, on average, in their early forties, of silicosis and the slow harm of mercury and lead. Their families pour out offerings of alcohol on the tunnel floors to a figure they call El Tio — Spanish for the uncle. He's a horned god they didn't have before the Spanish came. He lives in the mountain and rules the miners who enter it.

The city of Potosi today holds roughly two hundred thousand people, close to what it had at its 1611 peak. The mountain above it has been hollowed out. Its summit, geologists believe, sits several hundred feet lower than it did in 1545. It's one of the only mountains in the world on a UNESCO World Heritage list largely because of what human beings did to it.

The silver of Potosi built no monument. Spain spent it on armies that lost, and the bankers of Genoa and Augsburg poured it into ventures the world has long forgotten. The Chinese tax system drank it into the wider money of a state that would itself fall in the nineteenth century. The Manila Galleons rotted in Spanish dockyards. The patio yards at Potosi lie silent now, the mercury sealed under three centuries of tailings.

What the silver did leave behind is the modern world, in outline. The first trade route across the Pacific. The first global currency, the peso. The first wave of rising prices to cross whole continents. And the first colonial economy in which wealth pulled from one place made a third place rich by way of a second. Here, for the first time, the world saw the basic gears of how a global economy is meant to run, and how it's meant to break. It happened in the Andean cold, worked by an army of drafted miners under contract to a dynasty in Madrid. A dynasty that couldn't, in the end, keep the money.

The mountain broke the people who dug it. It broke the empire that owned it, and it broke the European wages it touched. And it built the world that came after.

Coloma, California, January 1848.

Three hundred years after Potosi, water was running down a tailrace in foothills the Spaniards had never reached.

CHAPTER EIGHT — THE CARPENTER AT THE SAWMILL

The men who find gold are rarely the men who keep it. And the land where it's found is seldom the better for having held it.

Coloma, California, January 1848 – 1880

James Marshall woke before dawn on January 24, 1848. He walked down from the small unfinished sawmill at Coloma to the tailrace below — the channel that carried water back to the American River once the mill had used it. And there, in the gravel at the bottom of the running water, he saw something yellow.

He was thirty-seven, a carpenter from New Jersey, lean and bearded, quiet even by frontier standards. For the last six months he had been building the sawmill for a Swiss land owner named John Sutter, who held title to fifty thousand acres of central California under a grant from the Mexican crown. The mill was nearly done. The night's water flow had cut the tailrace deeper, and Marshall was checking it when he saw the flakes.

He picked one up. It was the size of a fingernail and oddly heavy. He bit down on it. It bent without breaking — and if he remembered right from his old reading, only one metal did that. He gathered a few more and wrapped them in a cloth. Then he rode the forty-five miles back to Sutter's main estate to show his boss.

It would later be called one of the most consequential mornings of the century. Within a year and a half, three hundred thousand people from across the world would pour into the Sierra Nevada hills. California, which had been part of Mexico three years before and a thinly settled American land three months before, would become the thirty-first state of the Union. The men who had found the gold — Marshall and Sutter — would lose all they owned to the people who came after them. Both would die broke, in different cities a continent apart. And the gold itself would flow east in such floods that it helped pay for the Union army in the Civil War.

Marshall, that morning, didn't know any of this. He thought he had found gold.

John Sutter was forty-five years old in 1848, a heavy, restless Swiss who had reached California nine years before with big plans and bad debts. He had fled Switzerland in 1834 to escape the men he owed money to, leaving behind a wife and four children. He spent the next five years working his way west across North

America by a long, looping route — overland, then by sea by way of Hawaii and Alaska. In 1839 he sailed into the Sacramento Valley. There he talked the Mexican governor into handing him fifty thousand acres of land. The deal was that he settle it and bring it under Mexican law.

He named his land New Helvetia — New Switzerland. At its center he built a walled adobe trading post he called Sutter's Fort, where the Sacramento and American Rivers met. He kept cattle, ran flour mills, and traded with the overland settlers coming in from the United States. He also held a small private army of Native Californian workers who had little say in the matter. By 1847 he was the richest man in the north of California. He was one of its most powerful, too. The United States war with Mexico had ended a year before. The Treaty of Guadalupe Hidalgo was signed in February 1848 — ten days after Marshall picked up the flake. It would hand California from Mexican to American rule.

Sutter took the news, by every account, with dread. He knew at once what word like this would do. He swore Marshall and the four other sawmill workers to secrecy. Then he sent the gold flake to a Sacramento merchant named Sam Brannan. Brannan tested it and found it was gold of high purity. Sutter tried to get a legal grant of mineral rights to the land around the mill.

He asked the new American military governor for it. The governor said no. No such legal power was there, he said, in the messy gap between Mexican and American rule.

The secret held for about four months.

The man who broke it was Sam Brannan.

Brannan was a twenty-nine-year-old Mormon merchant who ran a general store at Sutter's Fort and a newspaper in San Francisco. He had tested the gold flake himself. And he saw, before almost anyone else, what the next few years were going to look like.

In April and May of 1848, Brannan quietly bought up every pickaxe, shovel, gold pan, mining cradle, and length of rope for sale in the north of California. He cornered the market on mining gear. Then, in mid-May, he went to San Francisco — at that point a small port town of about a thousand people. He walked through the streets holding a glass vial of gold dust over his head, shouting, Gold! Gold! Gold from the American River!

The town emptied within a week.

By the end of the month, the editor of one of San Francisco's two newspapers had to print a short notice. He was shutting the paper down, he wrote. There was no one left in the city to read it or write for it. Ships in the harbor were left empty by their crews, who swam ashore and walked east toward the foothills. Some of those ships sat at anchor for years, slowly rotting, their cargoes spoiling in the holds. Farmers left their fields. Soldiers walked off from their forts. Brannan, who hadn't dug a single ounce of gold himself, became California's first millionaire. He did it by selling at wild markups the goods he had cornered the market on a few weeks before.

In December of 1848, President James K. Polk made the find known, in his yearly message to Congress in Washington. The news reached the rest of the world over the next few weeks. By the spring of 1849, the largest peacetime move of people in modern times had begun.

The Forty-Niners — the wave of newcomers named for the year they came — arrived by every route there was, and every route had its own way of killing them. About a third came overland from the eastern United States. That was a four to six month trek across the Great Plains, the Rocky Mountains, and the Nevada deserts. It killed thousands along the way, from cholera, from mishaps, from cold. About a third came by ship around Cape Horn, a five to seven month voyage that took others by scurvy, shipwreck, and sickness. The rest crossed the Isthmus of Panama, picking their way over forty miles of mosquito-thick jungle on muleback. They braved yellow fever and malaria for the chance at a faster way through.

By the end of 1849, perhaps eighty thousand people had arrived. By 1855, the total was over three hundred thousand. They came from the eastern United States and Mexico, from South America, from China and Australia, from every corner of Europe. Almost all of them were men. Almost all of them were young. They came with no plan beyond reaching the gold fields and digging.

The gold fields ran along a strip of foothill country roughly three hundred miles long, on the western slope of the Sierra Nevada. A dozen rivers drained it, running out of the mountains toward the great central valley. The easy gold lay in the gravel beds of these rivers and their feeder creeks. It was placer gold, washed loose from upstream veins over millions of years, lying in nuggets and flakes among the river stones. In 1849 and 1850, a man with a tin pan, a strong back, and some luck could do well. He might pull more gold in a day than he could earn in a year as a hired hand back home.

For about two years, this was true.

By 1853, the easy gold was largely gone.

The shallow river gravels had been worked over by the hundreds of thousands who came. What was left lay deeper underground, locked in hard rock. Getting it out took money and machines and labor at a scale no single miner could handle. The men who had come west to dig now either worked for someone else's mining company or went home broke.

Two new ways took over. The first was hydraulic mining, honed in California in 1853. High-pressure water jets, fed by long sluice lines, were aimed at whole hillsides and washed them away. Every tree, every layer of soil, every cubic yard of dirt on top — all of it went, to lay bare the gold-bearing gravel below.

The way brought out a great deal of gold and tore up a great deal of land. Whole valleys were stripped to bedrock and forests were wiped out, and the loosened dirt and gravel ran downstream into the Sacramento and Feather Rivers. It raised their beds, flooded farms in the central valley, and choked shipping lanes all the way to San Francisco Bay. By the 1880s the harm was so plain that the California courts banned it in 1884 —

making it, by some accounts, the first big land-and-water law in American history.

The second way was mercury. Liquid mercury, dug from a mine in the coastal hills to the south, was used to bind with fine gold dust and pull it free of worthless sand. It was the same patio method the Spanish had used at Potosi, only smaller and worked by single men. Each ounce of California gold taken from the rivers took, on average, two ounces of mercury. Most of that mercury was lost into the water. A count of some ten million pounds of mercury went into the rivers and streams of the Sierra foothills during the gold rush years. It's still there. The Sacramento River carries mercury in its mud today at levels high enough to limit how often pregnant women in California are told they can eat the fish.

The Native Californians didn't survive the meeting.

In 1848, the Native people of California numbered somewhere between one hundred and fifty thousand and three hundred thousand. They were split among more than a hundred separate tribal groups, many of them small and clustered in single river valleys. Within twenty-five years, by 1873, that number had crashed to roughly thirty thousand — a drop of at least eighty in a hundred, and likely more.

Part of this fall was disease. Measles, smallpox, and the flu came with the miners and tore through people who had no shield against them. Part of it was being driven out. Mining wrecked the river homes that many California tribes leaned on for fish and acorn-bearing oaks. And part of it was outright killing. State and federal governments paid bounties for Native scalps. Mining camps put together armed raids against nearby villages. The first elected governor of California said in 1851 that a war of extermination will continue to be waged between the races, until the Indian race becomes extinct. For the most part, state and federal rulers did nothing to stop it.

What historians now call the California Genocide ran from roughly 1846 to 1873. The federal government owned up to it for the first time in 2019. The state of California did the same later the same year. None of it had been planned, exactly. It had simply happened. Three hundred thousand men with guns and picks had been let loose into a land where two hundred thousand other people already made their home.

The gold went east.

Most of the gold that came out of California in the rush years was shipped to San Francisco. There it was refined and struck into coins (the San Francisco Mint opened in 1854). From there it went by sea to New York and into the vaults of the East Coast banks. That gold paid for the great growth that shaped America in the late 1800s. It paid for the cross-country railroad, finished in 1869. It paid for the fast rise of factories in the northeast. And — most important of all — it paid for the Union side of the American Civil War.

When that war broke out in 1861, the Union held a clear money edge over the Confederacy. A large part of that edge was the California gold flow. Union paper dollars could be cashed in, in time, for California gold coin. Confederate money couldn't. The South was cut off, in effect, from foreign credit. The North could borrow on the strength of its steady gold inflows. The war that decided whether the United States would stay one country or split into two was paid for, in part, by men washing gravel in the American River.

By the late 1860s, the easy gold was twenty years gone, and California's trade had moved on to farming, lumber, and goods. Mining went on, but as a company business that hired wage workers, the way the lumber camps and the railroad gangs did. The men who had come for fortunes of their own had either gone home, or stayed and become farmers, or died.

The three men who had been at the start of it died poor, one after another.

James Marshall, the carpenter who had picked up the first flake, tried to mine the land around Coloma in the years right after his find. He turned up nothing worth keeping. By all accounts he wasn't a good miner. He had neither the patience nor the luck. Prospectors who flooded into Coloma chased him off the claims he tried to work, and he drifted from one job to another, and he drank. He died in a one-room cabin in Kelsey, California, in 1885, at the age of seventy-four. A small state pension he had been given was cut off seven years before that. They buried him in a hillside grave looking down on the spot where he had found the gold thirty-seven years earlier.

John Sutter watched his fifty thousand acres melt away under him in the years after 1848. The Forty-Niners squatted on his land and refused to leave. Hungry miners killed his cattle for food. His Native Californian workers, suddenly free to dig for themselves, walked away from the fort. By the autumn of 1849 he could ride across his own land and find hundreds of tents pitched in the meadows. His herds had grazed there the year before. It was ground he could no longer convince anyone he owned. His grain crops were trampled by stampedes of new arrivals. His sawmill at Coloma burned down in 1856.

He sued, again and again. In case after case, American courts ruled that his old Mexican land grant wasn't good under United States law. That was how the courts now read it after statehood. That grant had been the ground of his whole venture. By the mid-1850s his fortune was gone.

In 1865 he moved east to ask Congress for payment. He settled in a small Pennsylvania town and traveled each session to Washington with papers nobody read. He sat in the gallery of the House of Representatives as bills about him were set aside without debate. He died of a stroke in a hotel room in Washington, D.C., in 1880, two days after Congress broke up without taking up his plea for the seventeenth time.

Sam Brannan, the merchant who had run through the streets of San Francisco with his vial of gold dust, became California's first millionaire. He stayed the richest man in the state for over a decade. He put his money into land, into shipping, into a liquor company of his own. He bought up large parts of San Francisco. Then, in the early 1870s, he divorced his wife. The deal made him pay her half his fortune in cash — and sell off his holdings to do it. Most of what was left he lost in risky bets. He died in 1889 in a small town in San

Diego County, sleeping on a friend's couch, with almost nothing.

The three men had set the largest peacetime move of people in human history into motion. All three ended their lives in different cities, broke, with no lasting gain from what they had started.

The sawmill at Coloma is now a state historic park. A rebuilt version of the first sawmill stands on the bank of the American River, near the spot where the tailrace once ran. The original mill burned in 1856, and a small museum shows a few of Marshall's own belongings. Even now the river carries traces of mercury in its mud, and the nearby hills still show the scars of hydraulic mining. Bare rock canyons that the water cannons cut open are part of the guarded land today, walked over by hikers. And the children's children of the Native Californians who lived through the rush years run culture programs at the park, telling visitors what was here before them.

So in the end the gold gave nothing to the men who found it. They died penniless, one after another. The land was poisoned by the mercury used to pull the gold loose, and the rivers still carry that mercury today. Within twenty-five years, the people who had lived on the land were cut down by eighty percent. The gold itself went east, where it built the banks of New York and paid for the Union army in the Civil War. It never came back to the men who had washed it from the river.

On a hill above the old sawmill, a statue of Marshall still points toward the water. He's fixed there in bronze, one hand raised, gesturing forever at the place where he found the thing that destroyed his life.

CONCLUSION — THE METAL THAT WON'T LET GO

The metal has gotten busier in the twenty-first century, not less.

Between 2009 and 2024, the central banks of the world bought more gold, on balance, than in any like stretch since the Bretton Woods system — the postwar deal that tied world currencies to a gold-backed dollar — fell apart. Russia began piling it up in 2014, bracing for sanctions over its seizure of Crimea. China started buying again in 2018. The buying hit records in 2022.

On a Saturday morning in late February of that year, the chief reserve manager of the Bank of Russia opened his weekend report. About three hundred billion dollars of his bank's reserves had been frozen overnight. The money was held in dollars, euros, pounds, and yen across the central banks of the Western alliance, and those same governments had locked it. He couldn't move it. He couldn't spend it. He couldn't, in any real sense, even check the balance.

One thing he could still do. He could sell the gold the Bank of Russia held in its own vaults in Moscow — more than two thousand tons of it, built up over the previous fifteen years for exactly this day. It could be sold for any currency anyone in the world would pay. It was the one reserve asset the Western alliance couldn't reach, and every other non-Western central bank took the lesson within the same week.

In early 2025, the spot price of gold passed three thousand dollars an ounce for the first time in human history. The metal Croesus had stamped at Sardis was now worth ten times what it had been on the day President Nixon cut gold's tie to the dollar in 1971. For decades, gold mining companies had run on thin margins. Now they suddenly had more cash than they knew what to do with. New mines opened in places no one had mined for profit in a century: the deep shafts of South Africa, the high deserts of Nevada, the flooded dredges of the upper Amazon, the war zones of eastern Congo.

It's the Congo, in particular, that resembles the older stories.

In the eastern provinces of the Democratic Republic of Congo, a twelve-year-old boy climbs down a tunnel held up by rough timber and digs for gold in the dark for fourteen hours. He's paid in ore. A trader buys it and carries it across the border into Rwanda or Uganda, where it's mixed with legal ore and shipped to refiners in Dubai or Mumbai. From there it enters the world's gold supply, clean and legal. Each year, somewhere between fifty and one hundred and fifty tons of conflict gold reaches Western buyers — as much as the largest legal mines in the world put out in a year. Apple, Tesla, and the big Swiss refiners have been named again and again in studies of the supply chain. By all the evidence we have, they have kept buying.

In its essentials, the Congo gold trade is no different from the gold trades that paid for the Crusades, the Spanish conquest of the Americas, or the labor system at Potosi. The metal is dug out under conditions no one would choose for himself, by people who aren't paid anything close to what their work is worth. And it's sold to buyers who don't know — or don't much want to know — where it came from. The chain has changed on the surface: there are satellite phones now, customs forms, audit papers, and the killing is done with AK-47s instead of swords. The heart of it hasn't.

Some readers will close this book and decide the pattern is grim — that human beings would be better off without the metal that has done this to them for so long. In a way, that's the obvious response. It's also wrong. The metal isn't the thing doing it. The metal is inert. On its own, it has never killed anyone, started a war, sacked a city, or put a king to death. What has done all of that is the human power to invent value, to agree on it across the lines between cultures, and then to take the steps that the agreement demands.

That power isn't going to be unlearned. The agreement has held, with some breaks, since 547 BCE. Take gold away and the role would simply pass to some other thing: silver, salt, sugar, iron, oil, lithium, rare earths, cobalt, attention itself. The story of human beings and the things they have prized is the same story, whatever the thing happens to be. Gold is just the one that has been doing it the longest.

The metal is still in the vault under Liberty Street, behind the ninety-ton door. It's still in the central bank vault in Beijing and the Reserve Bank vault in Mumbai. It's still being lifted out of the deep shafts of Witwatersrand, the rivers of the upper Amazon, and the small dug pits of the eastern Congo. The price of an ounce of it, at the time this book went to press, was three thousand four hundred dollars.

What human beings do with the next ounce that comes out of the ground will look very much like what they have done with every ounce that has come out of the ground in the previous twenty-four hundred years.

The metal won't stop them. Nothing else has either.

ON SOURCES

The eight stories in this book are drawn from primary chronicles where they exist and from the modern historians who have made sense of those chronicles where they do not. A reader who wants to go further will find the following useful.

For Chapter One (Croesus), Herodotus's Histories, Book One, written in the fifth century BC, is the foundational source for the king of Lydia. From it come the visit of Solon, the test of the oracles, the camel-and-cavalry tactic at Sardis, and the pyre. The cementation process is discussed in Andrew Ramage and Paul Craddock, King Croesus' Gold (2000). David Schaps, The Invention of Coinage and the Monetization of Ancient Greece (2004), is the standard study of the Lydian innovation.

For Chapter Two (Cleopatra and Augustus), Suetonius's Life of Augustus (in The Twelve Caesars) is the source for the collapse in Roman interest rates. Plutarch's Life of Antony is the source for Antony's death, Cleopatra's negotiations, and the asp. The broader economic argument draws on Keith Hopkins and on the more recent quantitative work of Walter Scheidel.

For Chapter Three (the Fourth Crusade), Geoffrey of Villehardouin's Conquest of Constantinople is the Crusader source. Nicetas Choniates's O City of Byzantium (translated by Harry Magoulias in 1984) is the Byzantine source. Donald Queller and Thomas Madden, The Fourth Crusade: The Conquest of Constantinople (1997), is the standard modern study.

For Chapter Four (Mansa Musa), the Arab geographer al-Umari's Masalik al-absar fi mamalik al-amsar, written in Cairo in the 1330s on the basis of interviews with witnesses, is the primary source for the hajj and its effect on the Cairo gold market. Modern context can be found in François-Xavier Fauvelle, The Golden Rhinoceros (2018), and Michael Gomez, African Dominion (2018).

For Chapter Five (the Reformation), Roland Bainton's Here I Stand (1950) remains the most readable Luther biography. For the financial mechanics of the indulgence campaign and the Albrecht-Fugger transaction, Greg Steinmetz, The Richest Man Who Ever Lived: The Life and Times of Jacob Fugger (2015), is excellent. The indulgence accounts themselves survive in the Fugger Archives in Augsburg.

For Chapter Six (Atahualpa), Pedro Pizarro (Francisco's cousin), Relación del descubrimiento y conquista de los reinos del Perú (1571), is the eyewitness Spanish source. John Hemming, The Conquest of the Incas (1970, revised 1993), remains the definitive modern history.

For Chapter Seven (Potosí), Bartolomé Arzáns de Orsúa y Vela's eighteenth-century Historia de la Villa Imperial de Potosí is the encyclopedic colonial chronicle. Earl J. Hamilton, American Treasure and the Price Revolution in Spain, 1501–1650 (1934), established the silver-inflation argument and has been refined but not replaced. Kris Lane, Potosí: The Silver City That Changed the World (2019), is the best recent overview, and Nicholas Robins, Mercury, Mining, and Empire (2011), documents the human cost of the patio process and of Huancavelica.

For Chapter Eight (California), H. W. Brands, The Age of Gold (2002), and Susan Lee Johnson, Roaring Camp (2000), cover the rush itself. Albert Hurtado, John Sutter: A Life on the North American Frontier (2006), is the standard biography of Sutter. For the California Genocide, Benjamin Madley, An American Genocide (2016), is the comprehensive account.

The Introduction's description of the Federal Reserve gold vault draws on material published by the Federal Reserve Bank of New York. The Conclusion's account of central bank gold purchases draws on the annual reports of the World Gold Council and on reporting by the Financial Times, Reuters, and Bloomberg from 2022 through 2025.

Any errors in these eight stories are the author's. The historians named above bear no responsibility for the simplifications required to tell each chapter in roughly three thousand words.

END OF BOOK ONE

www.ingramcontent.com/pod-product-compliance
Lightning Source LLC
LaVergne TN
LVHW100322210926
848480LV00003B/1220